Javascript, jQuery, HTML and CSS Inteview Questions

Frontend Developer Interview

Second Edition

⌈2023⌉

Er.Vaibhav Singh Chuahan

Er.Vaibahv Singh Chuahan

Dedicating this book to the Universe within us.

वक्रतुण्ड महाकाय सूर्यकोटि समप्रभ।
निर्विघ्नं कुरु मे देव सर्वकार्येषु सर्वदा॥

Contents

Preface

This book covers Interview questions from the major topics that are asked in the interview for a Frontend Developer. Currently, it covers HTML, CSS, JavaScript, and jQuery. I will try to furthermore in upcoming editions of this book.

This book has questions for both freshers and experienced candidates. I have added almost all questions that I have come across in my carrier. I have faced many interviews myself, so I know the concerns of a candidate. On the contrary, I have also taken many interviews which make me familier with the other side too.

Although I have tried to cover many questions and answered them in berief.You are advised to have further knowledge by digging deep in case you are not familer with a concept as the explanation is short for many questions. For few most important sorts of questions I have given a long descrption which might help candidate further.In case of you find any typo or error in the book or if you want to contact me in case of any queries you can mail me directly on er_vaibhavsingh@yahoo.com

All the best for your Interview Preparations

Er. Vaibhav Singh Chauhan

14th May 2021

About Author

Er.Vaibhav Singh Chauhan is a software consultant and has wide experience working in the corporate environment. He has served as Project Leader and Team Lead in some reputed organizations working for Swedish, US, UK, Japanese, and Indian clients.

Website   : https://vaibonline.com

Email   : Er_VaibhavSingh@yahoo.com

JavaScript

1. What is JavaScript?

Answer: JavaScript is a high-level, interpreted programming language primarily used for building dynamic and interactive web pages. It is commonly embedded in HTML documents and executed by web browsers to enhance the functionality of web applications.

2. Explain the difference between `undefined` and `null` in JavaScript.

Answer: `undefined` is a variable that has been declared but not assigned a value. `null` is a value that represents the intentional absence of any object value. In other words, `undefined` is the absence of a value in a variable, while `null` is an assigned value that means "no value" or "empty."

3. What is the DOM (Document Object Model)?

Answer: The Document Object Model is a programming interface for web documents. It represents the structure of a document as a tree of objects, where each object corresponds to a part of the document, such as elements, attributes, and text. JavaScript can manipulate the DOM to dynamically change the content, structure, and style of a web page.

4. How does JavaScript handle asynchronous operations?

Answer: JavaScript uses mechanisms like callbacks, promises, and async/await to handle asynchronous operations. Callbacks are functions passed as arguments to another function and executed after the completion of an asynchronous operation. Promises provide a cleaner way to handle asynchronous code, and async/await is a syntax built on top of promises, making asynchronous code more readable and maintainable.

5. What is the difference between `let`, `const`, and `var` in JavaScript?

Answer:

  `var` is function-scoped, while `let` and `const` are block-scoped.

  `var` is hoisted to the top of its scope, while `let` and `const` are not.

  `const` is used for variables that should not be reassigned, while `let` is for variables that can be reassigned.

  `const` requires an initial value and cannot be declared without one.

6. Explain the concept of closures in JavaScript.

Answer: A closure is a function that has access to variables from its outer (enclosing) scope, even after the outer function has finished executing. Closures allow for the creation of private variables and help in implementing data encapsulation. They are often used to create functions with behavior that depends on their surrounding state.

7. What is the event loop in JavaScript?

Answer: The event loop is a core concept in JavaScript's concurrency model. It continuously checks the message queue for tasks to execute. It consists of two main components: the call stack and the message queue. Asynchronous operations, like callbacks and promises, are handled by the event loop, ensuring that they do not block the execution of other code.

8. What is the purpose of the `this` keyword in JavaScript?

Answer: The `this` keyword refers to the current execution context. Its value is determined by how a function is called. In a method, `this` refers to the object that the method is called on. In a standalone function, `this` typically refers to the global object (e.g., `window` in a browser). Arrow functions, however, do not have their own `this` and inherit it from the enclosing scope.

9. Explain the difference between synchronous and asynchronous programming.

Answer: Synchronous programming executes code sequentially, one statement at a time, and each statement must complete before the next one starts. Asynchronous programming allows tasks to be executed in the background, and the program can continue running other tasks without waiting for the asynchronous ones to finish. Asynchronous operations are often used for tasks like fetching data from a server or handling user input.

10. How does prototypal inheritance work in JavaScript?

Answer: In JavaScript, objects can inherit properties and methods from other objects through prototypal inheritance. Each object has a prototype object, and when a property or method is accessed on an object, JavaScript looks for it in the object itself. If not found, it looks in the prototype chain until the property or method is found or the end of the chain is reached. This mechanism allows for the creation of reusable and extensible code through object prototypes.

11.Explain the concept of hoisting in JavaScript.

Answer:Hoisting is a JavaScript behavior where variable and function declarations are moved to the top of their containing scope during the compilation phase. This means that you can use a variable or function before it is declared in the code. However, only the declarations are hoisted, not the initializations.

12.What are the differences between `==` and `===` in JavaScript?

Answer:`==` is the equality operator, and it performs type coercion, meaning it converts the operands to the same type before making the comparison. `===` is the strict equality operator, and it checks both the values and the types of the operands without performing type coercion. In general, it's recommended to use `===` to avoid unexpected type conversions.

13.What is the purpose of the `bind` method in JavaScript?

Answer:The `bind` method is used to create a new function that, when called, has its `this` keyword set to a specific value. It is often used to bind a function to a particular object, ensuring that the `this` value inside the function refers to that object. Additionally, `bind` can be used to partially apply arguments to a function.

14.Explain the concept of event delegation in JavaScript.

Answer:Event delegation is a pattern in which a single event listener is attached to a common ancestor of multiple elements. Instead of attaching an event listener to each individual element, the ancestor handles the events, and the event object's properties are used to identify the target element. This approach is more efficient, especially when dealing with a large number of dynamically created elements.

15.What is the purpose of the `map` function in JavaScript?

Answer:The `map` function is used to create a new array by applying a provided function to each element of an existing array. It does not modify the original array but returns a new one with the transformed values. This method is commonly used for tasks like transforming data, filtering elements, or performing calculations on each array element.

16.How does the `forEach` method differ from the `map` method?

Answer:Both `forEach` and `map` are methods for iterating over an array. The key difference is that `map` creates a new array with the results of applying a function to each element, while `forEach` simply iterates over the array and performs an action on each element. `forEach` does not return a new array and is typically used when you want to perform side effects on each element.

17.Explain the concept of the same-origin policy in the context of JavaScript.

Answer:The same-origin policy is a security measure implemented by web browsers to prevent scripts from making requests to a different domain than the one that served the original web page. This policy helps protect user data by ensuring that scripts running on a web page can only access resources on the same domain, preventing malicious activities such as cross-site request forgery (CSRF) and cross-site scripting (XSS) attacks.

18.What is a closure? Can you provide an example of its practical use?

Answer:A closure is a function that "closes over" variables from its outer (enclosing) scope, allowing it to access those variables even after the outer function has completed execution. An example of practical use is creating private variables in JavaScript. Here's an example:

```javascript
function createCounter() {
    let count = 0;

    return function() {
        count++;
        return count;
    };
}

const counter = createCounter();
console.log(counter()); // 1
console.log(counter()); // 2
```

In this example, the inner function returned by `createCounter` has access to the `count` variable, and its state is preserved between calls.

19.What is the purpose of the `apply` and `call` methods in JavaScript?

Answer:Both `apply` and `call` are methods that allow you to invoke a function with a specified `this` value, along with an array (for `apply`) or individual arguments (for `call`). These methods are often used to borrow methods from one object and apply them to another or to set the `this` value explicitly in a function call.

20.How does JavaScript handle memory management?

Answer:JavaScript uses automatic memory management, commonly known as garbage collection, to allocate and deallocate memory. The JavaScript engine automatically tracks and frees up memory that is no longer in use. Objects that are no longer referenced by any part of the program are eligible for garbage collection. Developers don't need to manually allocate or deallocate memory in JavaScript, but they should be mindful of creating memory leaks by unintentionally keeping references to objects that are no longer needed.

21.What is the Event Loop in JavaScript, and how does it work?

Answer:The Event Loop is a crucial part of JavaScript's concurrency model. It continuously checks the message queue for tasks to execute. The Event Loop consists of the call stack, which keeps track of the currently executing function, and the message queue, which holds tasks that are ready to be executed. Asynchronous operations, like callbacks and promises, are handled by the Event Loop, allowing non-blocking execution of code.

22.Explain the concept of Promises in JavaScript and how they differ from callbacks.

Answer:Promises are a way to handle asynchronous operations in a more readable and maintainable manner. They represent the eventual completion or failure of an asynchronous operation and allow chaining multiple asynchronous operations. Unlike callbacks, which can lead to callback hell (nested callbacks), promises provide a cleaner syntax and better error handling through `.then()` and `.catch()`.

23.What is the purpose of the `async` and `await` keywords in JavaScript?

Answer:The `async` keyword is used to define asynchronous functions, and the `await` keyword is used to pause the execution of an asynchronous function until a Promise is settled (resolved or rejected). Using `async` and `await` makes asynchronous code look more like synchronous code, improving readability and maintainability.

24.What is the purpose of the `let` and `const` keywords in modern JavaScript?

Answer:Both `let` and `const` are used to declare variables in JavaScript. `let` is block-scoped and allows for variable reassignment, while `const` is also block-scoped but is used for variables that should not be reassigned after initialization. `const` variables must be assigned a value at the time of declaration.

25.Explain the concept of callback functions and provide an example.

Answer:Callback functions are functions passed as arguments to other functions and are executed after the completion of a specific task. They are often used in asynchronous operations. Here's an example:

```javascript
function fetchData(callback) {
    // Simulating an asynchronous operation (e.g., fetching data from a server)
    setTimeout(function() {
        const data = 'Hello, World!';
        callback(data);
    }, 1000);
}

function processData(data) {
    console.log('Processed data:', data.toUpperCase());
}

// Usage
fetchData(processData);
```

26.What is the purpose of the `JSON.stringify()` and `JSON.parse()` methods in JavaScript?

Answer:`JSON.stringify()` is used to convert a JavaScript object into a JSON string, while `JSON.parse()` is used to parse a JSON string and convert it back into a JavaScript object. These methods are commonly used for data serialization and deserialization, especially when working with APIs.

27.Explain the concept of the "this" keyword in JavaScript and how it differs from other programming languages.

Answer:In JavaScript, the value of the `this` keyword is determined by how a function is called, not where it is declared. In a method, `this` refers to the object that the method is called on. In a standalone function, `this` refers to the global object (`window` in a browser). Arrow functions, however, don't have their own `this` and inherit it from the enclosing scope.

28.What is the purpose of the `typeof` operator in JavaScript?

Answer:The `typeof` operator is used to determine the type of a variable or expression. It returns a string indicating the data type, such as `"number"`, `"string"`, `"object"`, etc. It's important to note that `typeof null` returns `"object"`, which is considered a historical quirk in JavaScript.

29.Explain the concept of the Same-Origin Policy, and how can it be bypassed?

Answer:The Same-Origin Policy is a security measure that prevents scripts from making requests to a different domain than the one that served the original web page. Bypassing the Same-Origin Policy can be done using techniques like Cross-Origin Resource Sharing (CORS) or JSONP. However, these methods require server-side configuration or cooperation from the server to allow cross-origin requests.

30.What is the purpose of the `localStorage` and `sessionStorage` objects in JavaScript?

Answer:`localStorage` and `sessionStorage` are web storage options that allow developers to store key-value pairs locally on the user's browser. The data stored in `localStorage` persists even after the browser is closed and can be accessed across browser sessions. In contrast, data stored in `sessionStorage` is only available for the duration of the page session and is cleared when the session ends or the browser is closed.

31.What is the difference between `let` and `var` when declaring variables?

Answer: Both `let` and `var` are used to declare variables, but there are key differences. `let` is block-scoped, meaning it is only accessible within the block it's declared in, while `var` is function-scoped. Additionally, variables declared with `var` are hoisted to the top of their scope, while variables declared with `let` are not hoisted.

32.Explain the concept of the prototype chain in JavaScript.

Answer: The prototype chain is a mechanism in JavaScript that allows objects to inherit properties and methods from other objects. Each object has a prototype, and when a property or method is accessed on an object, JavaScript looks for it in the object itself. If not found, it continues to look in the prototype chain until the property or method is found or the end of the chain is reached.

33.What is the purpose of the `Array.prototype.map()` method? Provide an example.

Answer: The `map()` method is used to create a new array by applying a provided function to each element of an existing array. It does not modify the original array but returns a new one with the transformed values. Here's an example:

```javascript
const numbers = [1, 2, 3, 4, 5];

const squaredNumbers = numbers.map(function (num) {
    return num * num;
});

console.log(squaredNumbers); // Output: [1, 4, 9, 16, 25]
```

34.What is the purpose of the `Array.prototype.filter()` method? Provide an example.

Answer: The `filter()` method is used to create a new array with elements that pass a provided test function. It does not modify the original array. Here's an example:

```javascript
const numbers = [1, 2, 3, 4, 5];

const evenNumbers = numbers.filter(function (num) {
    return num % 2 === 0;
});

console.log(evenNumbers); // Output: [2, 4]
```

35.Explain the concept of callback hell and how it can be mitigated.

Answer: Callback hell, also known as the "pyramid of doom," occurs when multiple nested callbacks are used, leading to code that is hard to read and maintain. Promises and async/await are techniques that can be used to mitigate callback hell and make asynchronous code more readable and manageable.

36.What is the purpose of the `Object.keys()` method in JavaScript?

Answer: The `Object.keys()` method is used to retrieve an array of a given object's own enumerable property names (keys). It does not include properties from the object's prototype chain. This method is often used for iterating over an object's properties.

37.Explain the concept of memoization in JavaScript.

Answer: Memoization is an optimization technique where the results of expensive function calls are cached, so that if the same inputs occur again, the cached result is returned instead of recomputing the function. This can significantly improve the performance of functions with repeated or redundant calls.

38.What is the purpose of the `fetch` API in JavaScript? Provide an example.

Answer: The `fetch` API is used to make network requests (e.g., fetching data from a server) in a more modern and flexible way than traditional methods like XMLHttpRequest. Here's a simple example:

```javascript
fetch('https://api.example.com/data')
    .then(response => response.json())
    .then(data => console.log(data))
    .catch(error => console.error('Error:', error));
```

39.Explain the concept of a closure in JavaScript and provide an example.

Answer: A closure is a function that "closes over" variables from its outer (enclosing) scope, allowing it to access those variables even after the outer function has completed execution. Here's an example:

```javascript
function outerFunction() {
    let outerVariable = 'I am from the outer function';

    function innerFunction() {
        console.log(outerVariable);
    }

    return innerFunction;
}

const closureExample = outerFunction();
closureExample(); // Output: 'I am from the outer function'
```

40.What is the purpose of the `Object.create()` method in JavaScript?

Answer: The `Object.create()` method is used to create a new object with the specified prototype object and properties. It provides a way to implement prototypal inheritance in JavaScript. Here's a basic example:

```javascript
const personPrototype = {
    greet: function() {
        console.log('Hello!');
    }
};


const john = Object.create(personPrototype);
john.greet(); // Output: 'Hello!'
```

41.What is the purpose of the `try...catch` statement in JavaScript? Provide an example.

Answer: The `try...catch` statement is used for error handling in JavaScript. Code within the `try` block is executed, and if an exception is thrown, it is caught and handled in the `catch` block. Here's an example:

```javascript
try {
    // Code that might throw an exception
    throw new Error('This is an example error.');
} catch (error) {
    console.error('Error caught:', error.message);
}
```

42.Explain the concept of the "strict mode" in JavaScript.

Answer: Strict mode is a feature in JavaScript that helps catch common coding errors and prevents the use of certain error-prone features. It can be enabled for an entire script or a specific function by adding the directive `"use strict";` at the beginning. Strict mode improves code quality by making it less tolerant of potential errors.

43.What is the purpose of the `Object.freeze()` method in JavaScript?

Answer: The `Object.freeze()` method is used to freeze an object, making it immutable. Once an object is frozen, its properties cannot be added, modified, or removed. Any attempt to modify a frozen object will result in an error. This is useful when you want to ensure that an object remains unchanged.

44.Explain the concept of event bubbling in the context of the DOM.

Answer: Event bubbling is a phase in the DOM event propagation where the event starts from the target element and bubbles up through its ancestors in the DOM hierarchy. During event bubbling, the innermost element's event handler is executed first, followed by its ancestors' event handlers in order. This allows for capturing and handling events at different levels of the DOM hierarchy.

45.What is the purpose of the `localStorage` and `sessionStorage` objects in JavaScript? How do they differ?

Answer: Both `localStorage` and `sessionStorage` are used for client-side storage in web browsers. The key difference is that data stored in `localStorage` persists even after the browser is closed and can be accessed across browser sessions. On the other hand, data stored in `sessionStorage` is only available for the duration of the page session and is cleared when the session ends or the browser is closed.

46.Explain the concept of debouncing in JavaScript.

Answer: Debouncing is a technique used to ensure that time-consuming tasks do not fire so often, making them more efficient. It involves delaying the execution of a function until after a certain amount of time has passed since the last time the function was invoked. This is often used in scenarios like handling user input events, ensuring that a function is only called after the user has stopped typing for a specified duration.

47.What is the purpose of the `Object.keys()` method in JavaScript? How does it differ from `for...in` loop?

Answer: The `Object.keys()` method is used to retrieve an array of a given object's own enumerable property names (keys). It does not include properties from the object's prototype chain. In contrast, the `for...in` loop iterates over all enumerable properties, including those inherited from the prototype chain.

48.Explain the concept of the "Event Delegation" pattern in JavaScript.

Answer: Event delegation is a pattern where a single event listener is attached to a common ancestor of multiple elements. Instead of attaching an event listener to each individual element, the ancestor handles the events, and the event object's properties are used to identify the target element. This approach is more efficient, especially when dealing with a large number of dynamically created elements.

49.What is the purpose of the `Promise.all()` method in JavaScript? Provide an example.

Answer: `Promise.all()` is used to wait for all promises in an iterable (e.g., an array) to be fulfilled and returns a single promise that resolves with an array of the fulfilled values. If any of the promises are rejected, the `Promise.all()` promise is rejected. Here's an example:

```javascript
const promise1 = Promise.resolve('Hello');
const promise2 = 42;
const promise3 = new Promise((resolve, reject) => {
    setTimeout(resolve, 100, 'World');
});


Promise.all([promise1, promise2, promise3])
    .then(values => console.log(values))
    .catch(error => console.error('Error:', error));
```

50.Explain the concept of the "prototype" property in JavaScript and how it is related to inheritance.

Answer: In JavaScript, every object has a `prototype` property that refers to its parent object. When a property or method is accessed on an object, JavaScript looks for it in the object itself. If not found, it continues to look in the object's prototype, forming a prototype chain until the property or method is found or the end of the chain is reached. This mechanism is crucial for implementing inheritance in JavaScript.

51.Explain the concept of the Event Loop in JavaScript and how it helps in handling asynchronous operations.

Answer: The Event Loop is a mechanism in JavaScript that continuously checks the message queue for tasks to execute. It consists of the call stack, which keeps track of the currently executing function, and the message queue, which holds tasks that are ready to be executed. Asynchronous operations, like callbacks and promises, are handled by the Event Loop, ensuring that they do not block the execution of other code.

52.What is the purpose of the `Array.isArray()` method in JavaScript?

Answer: The `Array.isArray()` method is used to check whether a given value is an array. It returns `true` if the value is an array and `false` otherwise. This method is preferable to using `typeof` for checking arrays because `typeof` would return `'object'` for arrays.

53.Explain the concept of the "this" keyword in JavaScript and how it behaves in arrow functions.

Answer: The `this` keyword in JavaScript refers to the current execution context. In a method, `this` refers to the object that the method is called on. In a standalone function, `this` typically refers to the global object (`window` in a browser). However, arrow functions do not have their own `this`; they inherit it from the enclosing scope. This behavior makes arrow functions useful in scenarios where you want to preserve the `this` value from the surrounding context.

54. What is the purpose of the `Object.hasOwnProperty()` method in JavaScript? Provide an example.

Answer: The `hasOwnProperty()` method is used to check whether an object has a property with a specific key. It returns `true` if the object has the property directly defined on itself, and `false` otherwise. Here's an example:

```javascript
const person = { name: 'John', age: 30 };

console.log(person.hasOwnProperty('name')); // Output: true
console.log(person.hasOwnProperty('toString')); // Output: false
```

55. Explain the purpose of the JavaScript `Proxy` object and provide an example.

Answer: The `Proxy` object is used to create a proxy for another object, allowing custom behavior to be defined for fundamental operations (e.g., property access, assignment, function invocation). Here's a basic example:

```javascript
const target = { name: 'John' };

const handler = {
    get: function(target, property) {
        return property in target ? target[property] : 'Property not found';
    }
};

const proxy = new Proxy(target, handler);

console.log(proxy.name); // Output: 'John'
console.log(proxy.age); // Output: 'Property not found'
```

56. What is the purpose of the `Object.assign()` method in JavaScript? Provide an example.

Answer: The `Object.assign()` method is used to copy the values of all enumerable properties from one or more source objects to a target object. It returns the modified target object. Here's an example:

```javascript
const target = { a: 1, b: 2 };
const source = { b: 3, c: 4 };

const result = Object.assign(target, source);

console.log(result); // Output: { a: 1, b: 3, c: 4 }
```

57.Explain the concept of the "Promise race" in JavaScript.

Answer: The `Promise.race()` method is used to race multiple promises against each other. It takes an iterable of promises and returns a new promise that is fulfilled with the value of the first promise that resolves or rejects. This can be useful when you want to handle the result of the first promise that completes, regardless of whether it resolves or rejects.

58.What is the purpose of the `arguments` object in JavaScript functions? How does it differ from the `rest` parameter?

Answer: The `arguments` object is an array-like object available within the body of a function that contains the values of the arguments passed to the function. It is not available in arrow functions. On the other hand, the `rest` parameter (`...args`) allows a function to accept any number of arguments as an actual array. It is more flexible and easier to work with than the `arguments` object.

59.Explain the concept of the "Currying" function in JavaScript.

Answer: Currying is a functional programming concept where a function that takes multiple arguments is transformed into a sequence of functions, each taking a single argument. The result is a chain of partially applied functions that can be composed together. This technique allows for more modular and reusable code. Here's a basic example:

```javascript
function curry(fn) {
    return function curried(...args) {
        if (args.length >= fn.length) {
            return fn(...args);
        } else {
            return function(...moreArgs) {
                return curried(...args, ...moreArgs);
            };
        }
    };
}


const add = (a, b, c) => a + b + c;
const curriedAdd = curry(add);


console.log(curriedAdd(1)(2)(3)); // Output: 6
```

60. What is the purpose of the `typeof` operator in JavaScript, and what are its limitations?

Answer: The `typeof` operator is used to determine the type of a variable or expression. It returns a string indicating the data type, such as `"number"`, `"string"`, `"object"`, etc. However, `typeof` has limitations, such as returning `"object"` for arrays and `null`. For more accurate type checking, other methods like `Array.isArray()` or checking for `null` explicitly are recommended.

61. What is the purpose of the `localStorage` and `sessionStorage` objects in JavaScript? How do they differ?

Answer: Both `localStorage` and `sessionStorage` are used for client-side storage in web browsers. The key difference is that data stored in `localStorage` persists even after the browser is closed and can be accessed across browser sessions. In contrast, data stored in `sessionStorage` is only available for the duration of the page session and is cleared when the session ends or the browser is closed.

62. Explain the concept of debouncing in JavaScript.

Answer: Debouncing is a technique used to ensure that time-consuming tasks do not fire so often, making them more efficient. It involves delaying the execution of a function until after a certain amount of time has passed since the last time the function was invoked. This is often used in scenarios like handling user input events, ensuring that a function is only called after the user has stopped typing for a specified duration.

63. What is the purpose of the JavaScript `Proxy` object and provide an example.

Answer: The `Proxy` object is used to create a proxy for another object, allowing custom behavior to be defined for fundamental operations (e.g., property access, assignment, function invocation). Here's a basic example:

```javascript
const target = { name: 'John' };

const handler = {
    get: function(target, property) {
        return property in target ? target[property] : 'Property not found';
    }
};

const proxy = new Proxy(target, handler);

console.log(proxy.name); // Output: 'John'
console.log(proxy.age); // Output: 'Property not found'
```

64. What is the purpose of the `Object.assign()` method in JavaScript? Provide an example.

Answer: The `Object.assign()` method is used to copy the values of all enumerable properties from one or more source objects to a target object. It returns the modified target object. Here's an example:

```
const target = { a: 1, b: 2 };
const source = { b: 3, c: 4 };

const result = Object.assign(target, source);

console.log(result); // Output: { a: 1, b: 3, c: 4 }
```

65. Explain the concept of the "Promise race" in JavaScript.

Answer: The `Promise.race()` method is used to race multiple promises against each other. It takes an iterable of promises and returns a new promise that is fulfilled with the value of the first promise that resolves or rejects. This can be useful when you want to handle the result of the first promise that completes, regardless of whether it resolves or rejects.

66. What is the purpose of the `arguments` object in JavaScript functions? How does it differ from the `rest` parameter?

Answer: The `arguments` object is an array-like object available within the body of a function that contains the values of the arguments passed to the function. It is not available in arrow functions. On the other hand, the `rest` parameter (`...args`) allows a function to accept any number of arguments as an actual array. It is more flexible and easier to work with than the `arguments` object.

67. Explain the concept of the "Currying" function in JavaScript.

Answer: Currying is a functional programming concept where a function that takes multiple arguments is transformed into a sequence of functions, each taking a single argument. The result is a chain of partially applied functions that can be composed together. This technique allows for more modular and reusable code. Here's a basic example:

```javascript
function curry(fn) {
    return function curried(...args) {
        if (args.length >= fn.length) {
            return fn(...args);
        } else {
            return function(...moreArgs) {
                return curried(...args, ...moreArgs);
            };
        }
    };
}

const add = (a, b, c) => a + b + c;
const curriedAdd = curry(add);

console.log(curriedAdd(1)(2)(3)); // Output: 6
```

68. What is the purpose of the `typeof` operator in JavaScript, and what are its limitations?

Answer: The `typeof` operator is used to determine the type of a variable or expression. It returns a string indicating the data type, such as `"number"`, `"string"`, `"object"`, etc. However, `typeof` has limitations, such as returning `"object"` for arrays and `null`. For more accurate type checking, other methods like `Array.isArray()` or checking for `null` explicitly are recommended.

69. Explain the concept of the "Promise.allSettled()" method in JavaScript.

Answer: The `Promise.allSettled()` method is used to wait for all promises in an iterable (e.g., an array) to settle (either fulfill or reject). It returns a new promise that is fulfilled with an array of objects, each representing the outcome of the corresponding promise. This method is useful when you want to handle the result of all promises, regardless of whether they resolved or rejected.

70. What is the purpose of the `Array.prototype.reduce()` method in JavaScript? Provide an example.

Answer: The `reduce()` method is used to reduce an array to a single value by applying a function to each element and accumulating the result. The accumulated result is often referred to as the "accumulator." Here's an example that calculates the sum of an array:

```javascript
const numbers = [1, 2, 3, 4, 5];

const sum = numbers.reduce(function (accumulator, current) {
    return accumulator + current;
}, 0);

console.log(sum); // Output: 15
```

71.Explain the concept of the "Memoization" pattern in JavaScript.

Answer:Memoization is an optimization technique where the results of expensive function calls are cached, so that if the same inputs occur again, the cached result is returned instead of recomputing the function. This can significantly improve the performance of functions with repeated or redundant calls.

72.What is the purpose of the `WeakMap` and `WeakSet` objects in JavaScript?

Answer:`WeakMap` and `WeakSet` are collections in JavaScript that allow only weak references to the keys or values they store. In a `WeakMap`, keys must be objects, and they are held weakly, meaning they won't prevent garbage collection. Similarly, in a `WeakSet`, values must be objects and are held weakly. This makes them useful for scenarios where you want to associate data with objects without preventing them from being garbage collected.

73.Explain the concept of the "Spread Syntax" in JavaScript.

Answer:The spread syntax (`...`) is used to spread elements of an iterable (e.g., an array) or properties of an object into a new array or object. It allows for easy duplication and merging of arrays and objects. Here are a couple of examples:

```javascript
// Spread in arrays
const arr1 = [1, 2, 3];
const arr2 = [...arr1, 4, 5];

console.log(arr2); // Output: [1, 2, 3, 4, 5]

// Spread in objects
const obj1 = { a: 1, b: 2 };
const obj2 = { ...obj1, c: 3 };

console.log(obj2); // Output: { a: 1, b: 2, c: 3 }
```

74.What is the purpose of the `requestAnimationFrame` function in JavaScript?

Answer:The `requestAnimationFrame` function is used to schedule a function to be called before the next repaint of the browser. It is often used for smooth and efficient animations in web applications. Compared to using `setTimeout` or `setInterval` for animations, `requestAnimationFrame` provides better performance by syncing with the browser's rendering pipeline.

75.Explain the concept of the "Fetch API" in JavaScript and how it differs from XMLHttpRequest.

Answer:The Fetch API is a modern interface for making network requests (e.g., fetching data from a server) in JavaScript. It provides a more flexible and powerful way to handle HTTP requests compared to the older XMLHttpRequest. Fetch returns promises, making it easier to work with asynchronous code, and it has a simpler and cleaner syntax.

76.What is the purpose of the `Array.from()` method in JavaScript? Provide an example.

Answer:The `Array.from()` method is used to create a new array from an iterable or array-like object. It takes a mapping function as an optional argument. Here's an example:

```javascript
const set = new Set([1, 2, 3]);
const array = Array.from(set, x => x * x);

console.log(array); // Output: [1, 4, 9]
```

77.Explain the concept of "Hoisting" in JavaScript.

Answer:Hoisting is a JavaScript behavior where variable and function declarations are moved to the top of their containing scope during the compilation phase. This allows variables and functions to be used before they are declared in the code. However, only the declarations are hoisted, not the initializations.

78.What is the purpose of the `Set` object in JavaScript? How does it differ from an array?

Answer:The `Set` object is a collection of unique values, and it does not allow duplicate values. It is useful when you need to work with a distinct set of values. Unlike arrays, sets do not have an order, and their elements cannot be accessed by index. Sets provide methods like `add`, `delete`, and `has` for managing elements.

79.Explain the concept of the "Generator" function in JavaScript.

Answer:A Generator function is a special type of function in JavaScript that allows you to pause its execution and later resume it. It uses the `yield` keyword to produce a sequence of values. Generator functions are defined using function* syntax and can be iterated over using a `for...of` loop. Here's a simple example:

```javascript
function* generateSequence() {
    yield 1;
    yield 2;
    yield 3;
}

const generator = generateSequence();

for (const value of generator) {
    console.log(value); // Output: 1, 2, 3
}
```

80.What is the purpose of the `Object.freeze()` method in JavaScript?

Answer:The `Object.freeze()` method is used to freeze an object, making it immutable. Once an object is frozen, its properties cannot be added, modified, or removed. Any attempt to modify a frozen object will result in an error. This is useful when you want to ensure that an object remains unchanged.

81.Explain the concept of the "IIFE" (Immediately Invoked Function Expression) pattern in JavaScript.

Answer: IIFE is a design pattern in JavaScript where a function is declared and executed immediately after its creation. It is often used to create a private scope for variables, preventing them from polluting the global scope. Here's an example:

```javascript
(function() {
    // IIFE body
    var privateVariable = 'I am private';
    console.log(privateVariable);
})();
```

82.What is the purpose of the JavaScript `Map` object, and how does it differ from a regular object?

Answer: The `Map` object is a collection of key-value pairs where both the keys and values can be of any data type. It provides methods for easy manipulation and iteration. Unlike a regular object, a `Map` allows any data type as a key and maintains the order of insertion.

83.Explain the concept of the "Promise.finally()" method in JavaScript.

Answer: The `Promise.finally()` method is used to specify a function that will be called when a promise is settled (either fulfilled or rejected). This is useful for cleanup operations that need to be performed regardless of the promise's outcome. The `finally` block is executed once the promise is settled.

```javascript
const promise = new Promise((resolve, reject) => {
    // Promise logic
    resolve('Success');
});

promise
    .then(result => console.log(result))
    .catch(error => console.error(error))
    .finally(() => console.log('Finally block executed'));
```

84.What is the purpose of the `Object.values()` method in JavaScript? Provide an example.

Answer: The `Object.values()` method is used to retrieve an array of a given object's own enumerable property values. It does not include values from the object's prototype chain. Here's an example:

```javascript
const person = { name: 'John', age: 30, occupation: 'Developer' };
const values = Object.values(person);

console.log(values); // Output: ['John', 30, 'Developer']
```

85.Explain the concept of the "Module Pattern" in JavaScript.

Answer: The Module Pattern is a design pattern in JavaScript that encapsulates private and public members within a module, providing a way to organize and structure code. It typically involves creating a closure to enclose private variables and functions, exposing only the necessary functionality through a public API.

```javascript
const module = (function() {
    // Private variable
    let privateVariable = 'I am private';


    // Private function
    function privateFunction() {
        console.log('Private function');
    }


    // Public API
    return {
        publicVariable: 'I am public',
        publicFunction: function() {
            console.log('Public function');
            privateFunction(); // Accessing private function
        }
    };
})();

console.log(module.publicVariable);
module.publicFunction();
```

86.What is the purpose of the `String.prototype.trim()` method in JavaScript?

Answer: The `trim()` method is used to remove whitespace (spaces, tabs, and newlines) from both ends of a string. It does not modify the original string but returns a new one with leading and trailing whitespace removed.

```javascript
const text = '   Hello, World!   ';
const trimmedText = text.trim();


console.log(trimmedText); // Output: 'Hello, World!'
```

87.Explain the concept of the "Event Delegation" pattern in JavaScript.

Answer: Event delegation is a pattern where a single event listener is attached to a common ancestor of multiple elements. Instead of attaching an event listener to each individual element, the ancestor handles the events, and the event object's properties are used to identify the target element. This approach is more efficient, especially when dealing with a large number of dynamically created elements.

88.What is the purpose of the `String.prototype.split()` method in JavaScript? Provide an example.

Answer: The `split()` method is used to split a string into an array of substrings based on a specified delimiter. Here's an example:

```javascript
const sentence = 'This is a sample sentence';
const words = sentence.split(' ');


console.log(words); // Output: ['This', 'is', 'a', 'sample', 'sentence']
```

89.Explain the concept of "Currying" in JavaScript, and provide an example using arrow functions.

Answer: Currying is a technique where a function with multiple arguments is transformed into a sequence of functions, each taking a single argument. Arrow functions can be used for concise currying. Here's an example:

```javascript
const curry = (fn, ...args) =>
    args.length >= fn.length
        ? fn(...args)
        : (...moreArgs) => curry(fn, ...args, ...moreArgs);

const add = (a, b, c) => a + b + c;
const curriedAdd = curry(add);


console.log(curriedAdd(1)(2)(3)); // Output: 6
```

90. What is the purpose of the `event.preventDefault()` method in JavaScript?

Answer: The `event.preventDefault()` method is used to prevent the default behavior associated with an event. For example, it is commonly used in event handlers for form submissions to prevent the page from being refreshed when the form is submitted. This method is essential for controlling the behavior of events.

91. What is the purpose of the `Object.seal()` method in JavaScript?

Answer: The `Object.seal()` method is used to seal an object, preventing new properties from being added and marking all existing properties as non-configurable. While the values of existing properties can still be changed, their descriptors cannot be modified. This provides a level of immutability to the object's structure.

```javascript
const obj = { name: 'John', age: 30 };

Object.seal(obj);
```

```
// Adding a new property (will have no effect in strict mode)

obj.gender = 'Male';


// Modifying an existing property is allowed

obj.age = 31;


// Deleting an existing property is not allowed

delete obj.name; // Returns false in strict mode


console.log(obj); // Output: { name: 'John', age: 31 }
```

92.Explain the concept of the "Event Loop" in JavaScript. How does it handle asynchronous tasks?

Answer: The Event Loop is a mechanism in JavaScript that continuously checks the message queue for tasks to execute. It consists of the call stack, which keeps track of the currently executing function, and the message queue, which holds tasks that are ready to be executed. Asynchronous tasks, such as those involving callbacks and promises, are offloaded to the browser's APIs. Once completed, these tasks are placed in the message queue, and the Event Loop ensures they are executed at the appropriate time.

93.What is the purpose of the `Array.prototype.findIndex()` method in JavaScript? Provide an example.

Answer: The `findIndex()` method is used to find the index of the first element in an array that satisfies a provided testing function. If no element satisfies the condition, -1 is returned. Here's an example:

```javascript
const numbers = [1, 2, 3, 4, 5];
const index = numbers.findIndex(num => num > 2);

console.log(index); // Output: 2 (index of the first element greater than 2)
```

94.Explain the concept of the "Object Destructuring" in JavaScript.

Answer: Object destructuring is a feature in JavaScript that allows you to extract values from objects and bind them to variables using a concise syntax. It is particularly useful when working with objects with many properties. Here's an example:

```javascript
const person = { name: 'Alice', age: 25, country: 'USA' };
const { name, age } = person;

console.log(name, age); // Output: 'Alice' 25
```

95.What is the purpose of the `Function.prototype.bind()` method in JavaScript? Provide an example.

Answer: The `bind()` method is used to create a new function that, when called, has its `this` keyword set to a specific value, provided as an argument. It is often used to bind a function to a specific context. Here's an example:

```javascript
const greet = function() {
    console.log(`Hello, ${this.name}!`);
};

const person = { name: 'John' };
const greetJohn = greet.bind(person);

greetJohn(); // Output: 'Hello, John!'
```

96.Explain the concept of the "Observer Pattern" in JavaScript.

Answer: The Observer Pattern is a behavioral design pattern where an object, known as the subject, maintains a list of its dependents, known as observers, that are notified of any changes in the subject's state. This pattern is commonly used to implement distributed event handling systems, such as those found in many GUI frameworks.

97.What is the purpose of the `Symbol` data type in JavaScript? Provide an example.

Answer: The `Symbol` data type is used to create unique values that can be used as property keys for objects. Symbols are guaranteed to be unique, preventing accidental property name collisions. Here's an example:

```javascript
const mySymbol = Symbol('My Symbol');
const obj = {
    [mySymbol]: 'This is a symbol property'
};

console.log(obj[mySymbol]); // Output: 'This is a symbol property'
```

98.Explain the concept of the "Two-Factor Authentication (2FA)" and how it can be implemented in JavaScript.

Answer: Two-Factor Authentication (2FA) is a security mechanism where access is granted only after presenting two different authentication factors: something you know (e.g., a password) and something you have (e.g., a mobile app-generated code). In JavaScript, 2FA can be implemented using libraries like `speakeasy` or through Time-based One-Time Passwords (TOTPs).

99.What is the purpose of the `Array.prototype.some()` method in JavaScript? Provide an example.

Answer: The `some()` method is used to test whether at least one element in the array satisfies the provided testing function. It returns `true` if any element passes the test; otherwise, it returns `false`. Here's an example:

```javascript
const numbers = [1, 2, 3, 4, 5];
const hasEven = numbers.some(num => num % 2 === 0);


console.log(hasEven); // Output: true (because 2 is even)
```

100.Explain the concept of "Callback Hell" in JavaScript and how it can be mitigated.

 Answer: Callback Hell, also known as the "Pyramid of Doom," refers to a situation where multiple nested callbacks make the code difficult to read and maintain. This commonly occurs with asynchronous operations. To mitigate Callback Hell, developers can use techniques like modularization, named functions, Promises, or async/await syntax to improve code readability and manage the flow of asynchronous operations.

101.What is the purpose of the `Array.prototype.flat()` method in JavaScript? Provide an example.

Answer: The `flat()` method is used to flatten nested arrays by a specified depth. It creates a new array with all sub-array elements concatenated into it recursively up to the specified depth. Here's an example:

```javascript
const nestedArray = [1, [2, [3, [4]]]];
const flattenedArray = nestedArray.flat(2);


console.log(flattenedArray); // Output: [1, 2, 3, 4]
```

102.Explain the concept of "Closure" in JavaScript.

Answer: A closure is a function that has access to variables from its outer (enclosing) scope, even after the outer function has finished executing. This allows the inner function to "remember" and access those variables. Closures are a fundamental concept in JavaScript and are commonly used for creating private variables and implementing data encapsulation.

```javascript
function outer() {
    const outerVar = 'I am from outer';

    function inner() {
        console.log(outerVar);
    }

    return inner;
}

const closureFunction = outer();
closureFunction(); // Output: 'I am from outer'
```

103.What is the purpose of the `Object.create()` method in JavaScript? Provide an example.

Answer: The `Object.create()` method is used to create a new object with the specified prototype object and properties. It allows for prototypal inheritance without the need for constructor functions. Here's an example:

```javascript
const personPrototype = {
    greet: function() {
        console.log(`Hello, ${this.name}!`);
    }
};


const person = Object.create(personPrototype);
person.name = 'John';
person.greet(); // Output: 'Hello, John!'
```

104.Explain the concept of "Promises" in JavaScript and how they help with asynchronous programming.

Answer: Promises are objects representing the eventual completion or failure of an asynchronous operation. They provide a cleaner way to handle asynchronous code compared to callbacks. A promise can be in one of three states: pending, fulfilled, or rejected. Developers can attach `.then()` and `.catch()` handlers to handle the success or failure of the asynchronous operation.

```javascript
const fetchData = () => {
    return new Promise((resolve, reject) => {
        // Asynchronous operation (e.g., API call)
        const data = ...;

        if (data) {
            resolve(data); // Operation succeeded
        } else {
            reject('Error'); // Operation failed
        }
    });
};


fetchData()
    .then(result => console.log(result))
    .catch(error => console.error(error));
```

105.What is the purpose of the `Array.prototype.every()` method in JavaScript? Provide an example.

Answer: The `every()` method is used to test whether all elements in an array pass a provided testing function. It returns `true` if all elements pass the test; otherwise, it returns `false`. Here's an example:

```javascript
const numbers = [2, 4, 6, 8, 10];
const allEven = numbers.every(num => num % 2 === 0);

console.log(allEven); // Output: true (all elements are even)
```

106.Explain the concept of "Web Workers" in JavaScript.

Answer: Web Workers are a feature in JavaScript that allows the execution of scripts in the background, separate from the main thread. They enable multi-threading in web applications, providing a way to perform time-consuming tasks without affecting the responsiveness of the user interface. Communication between the main thread and a Web Worker is achieved using a messaging system.

107.What is the purpose of the `String.prototype.includes()` method in JavaScript? Provide an example.

Answer: The `includes()` method is used to determine whether a string contains another string. It returns `true` if the specified substring is found; otherwise, it returns `false`. Here's an example:

```javascript
const sentence = 'This is a sample sentence';
const containsWord = sentence.includes('sample');

console.log(containsWord); // Output: true
```

108.Explain the concept of "Cross-Origin Resource Sharing (CORS)" in the context of JavaScript and web development.

Answer: CORS is a security feature implemented by web browsers to control access to resources on a different origin (domain, protocol, or port). It restricts web pages from making requests to a different domain than the one that served the web page. To enable cross-origin requests, servers must include the appropriate CORS headers in their responses.

109.What is the purpose of the `Array.prototype.reduceRight()` method in JavaScript? Provide an example.

Answer: The `reduceRight()` method is similar to `reduce()`, but it processes the array from right to left. It applies a function against an accumulator and each element in reverse order to reduce the array to a single value. Here's an example:

```javascript
const numbers = [1, 2, 3, 4, 5];
const sum = numbers.reduceRight((acc, num) => acc + num, 0);

console.log(sum); // Output: 15 (5 + 4 + 3 + 2 + 1)
```

110.Explain the concept of "Memoization" and how it can be implemented in JavaScript.

Answer: Memoization is an optimization technique where the results of expensive function calls are cached, so that if the same inputs occur again, the cached result is returned instead of recomputing the function. Memoization can be implemented manually using an object to store cached results or by using memoization libraries like `lodash.memoize`.

```javascript
function expensiveOperation(n) {
    // Expensive computation
    return n * n;
}


const memoizedOperation = (function() {
    const cache = {};


    return function(n) {
        if (cache[n] === undefined) {
            cache[n] = expensiveOperation(n);
        }
        return cache[n];
    };
})();


console.log(memoizedOperation(5)); // Output: 25 (computed)
console.log(memoizedOperation(5)); // Output: 25 (cached)
```

111.What is the purpose of the `Array.prototype.slice()` method in JavaScript? Provide an example.

Answer: The `slice()` method is used to extract a portion of an array and returns a new array. It takes two arguments, the starting index and the ending index (not inclusive). Here's an example:

```javascript
const numbers = [1, 2, 3, 4, 5];

const slicedArray = numbers.slice(1, 4);
```

```
console.log(slicedArray); // Output: [2, 3, 4]

```

112.Explain the concept of "Event Bubbling" in JavaScript.

Answer: Event Bubbling is a phase in the event propagation model where an event starts from the target element that triggered the event and bubbles up through its ancestors in the DOM hierarchy. This allows parent elements to also handle the event. Event listeners attached to parent elements will be triggered after the event has been processed by the target and its ancestors.

113.What is the purpose of the `Object.keys()` method in JavaScript? Provide an example.

Answer: The `Object.keys()` method is used to retrieve an array of a given object's own enumerable property names. It does not include properties from the object's prototype chain. Here's an example:

```javascript
const person = { name: 'Alice', age: 25, country: 'USA' };
const keys = Object.keys(person);

console.log(keys); // Output: ['name', 'age', 'country']
```

114.Explain the concept of "Polymorphism" in JavaScript.

Answer: Polymorphism is a concept in object-oriented programming that allows objects of different types to be treated as objects of a common type. In JavaScript, polymorphism can be achieved through method overriding or by implementing interfaces. For example, different objects may have a common method with the same name but different implementations.

```javascript
class Shape {
    area() {
        return 0;
    }
}

class Circle extends Shape {
    constructor(radius) {
        super();
        this.radius = radius;
    }

    area() {
        return Math.PI * this.radius ** 2;
    }
}

class Rectangle extends Shape {
    constructor(width, height) {
        super();
        this.width = width;
        this.height = height;
    }

    area() {
        return this.width * this.height;
    }
}
```

```javascript
const circle = new Circle(5);
const rectangle = new Rectangle(4, 6);


console.log(circle.area()); // Output: 78.54
console.log(rectangle.area()); // Output: 24
```

115.What is the purpose of the `String.prototype.charCodeAt()` method in JavaScript? Provide an example.

Answer: The `charCodeAt()` method is used to return the Unicode code of the character at a specified index in a string. Here's an example:

```javascript
const str = 'Hello';
const charCode = str.charCodeAt(1);

console.log(charCode); // Output: 101 (Unicode code for 'e')
```

116.Explain the concept of "Functional Programming" in JavaScript.

Answer: Functional Programming is a programming paradigm that treats computation as the evaluation of mathematical functions and avoids changing state and mutable data. In JavaScript, functional programming concepts include higher-order functions, pure functions, immutability, and avoiding side effects.

117.What is the purpose of the `decodeURI()` and `decodeURIComponent()` functions in JavaScript? Provide examples.

Answer: The `decodeURI()` and `decodeURIComponent()` functions are used to decode Uniform Resource Identifiers (URIs) and URI components, respectively. They are used to convert percent-encoded characters back to their original form. Here are examples:

```javascript
const encodedURI = 'https%3A%2F%2Fwww.example.com%2Fpage%3Fid%3D123';
const decodedURI = decodeURI(encodedURI);


console.log(decodedURI);
// Output: 'https://www.example.com/page?id=123'
```


```javascript
const encodedComponent = 'Hello%2C%20World%21';
const decodedComponent = decodeURIComponent(encodedComponent);


console.log(decodedComponent);
// Output: 'Hello, World!'
```

118. Explain the concept of "ESLint" in the context of JavaScript development.

Answer: ESLint is a popular static code analysis tool for identifying and fixing problems in JavaScript code. It helps maintain a consistent coding style, identifies potential errors, and enforces best practices. ESLint configurations can be customized based on project-specific rules, and it can be integrated into development workflows to catch issues early.

119. What is the purpose of the `Array.prototype.splice()` method in JavaScript? Provide an example.

Answer: The `splice()` method is used to change the contents of an array by removing or replacing existing elements and/or adding new elements in place. It modifies the array and returns an array containing the removed elements. Here's an example:

```javascript
const numbers = [1, 2, 3, 4, 5];
const removedElements = numbers.splice(2, 2, 6, 7);


console.log(numbers); // Output: [1, 2, 6, 7, 5]
console.log(removedElements); // Output: [3, 4]
```

120.Explain the concept of "Scoped CSS" in the context of JavaScript frameworks like React.

Answer: Scoped CSS refers to a technique where the styles defined for a component are encapsulated and apply only to that specific component. In frameworks like React, this is achieved using techniques such as CSS Modules or styled-components. Scoped CSS helps avoid global style pollution and makes it easier to manage styles for individual components.

121.What is the purpose of the `Object.assign()` method in JavaScript? Provide an example.

-Answer:The `Object.assign()` method is used to copy the values of all enumerable properties from one or more source objects to a target object. It modifies the target object and returns it. Here's an example:

```javascript
const target = { a: 1, b: 2 };
const source = { b: 3, c: 4 };

const result = Object.assign(target, source);

console.log(result); // Output: { a: 1, b: 3, c: 4 }
```

122.Explain the concept of "Pure Functions" in JavaScript.

-Answer:Pure Functions are functions that, given the same input, will always return the same output and have no side effects. They don't modify external state or rely on external state changes. Pure Functions are a key concept in functional programming and contribute to code predictability and testability.

```javascript
// Pure function example
function add(a, b) {
    return a + b;
}


const result = add(3, 4); // Output: 7
```

123. What is the purpose of the `Array.prototype.findIndex()` method in JavaScript? Provide an example.

   -Answer:The `findIndex()` method is used to find the index of the first element in an array that satisfies a provided testing function. If no element satisfies the condition, -1 is returned. Here's an example:

```javascript
const numbers = [1, 2, 3, 4, 5];
const index = numbers.findIndex(num => num > 2);

console.log(index); // Output: 2 (index of the first element greater than 2)
```

124. Explain the concept of "Currying" in JavaScript, and provide an example.

   -Answer:Currying is a technique in functional programming where a function with multiple arguments is transformed into a sequence of functions, each taking a single argument. This allows for partial application of the function. Here's an example:

```javascript
// Currying example
function curryAdd(a) {
    return function(b) {
        return a + b;
    };
}


const add5 = curryAdd(5);
const result = add5(3); // Output: 8
```

125.What is the purpose of the `Array.prototype.map()` method in JavaScript? Provide an example.

-Answer:The `map()` method is used to create a new array by applying a provided function to each element of an existing array. It does not modify the original array. Here's an example:

```javascript
const numbers = [1, 2, 3, 4, 5];
const squaredNumbers = numbers.map(num => num * num);

console.log(squaredNumbers); // Output: [1, 4, 9, 16, 25]
```

126.Explain the concept of "Object-Oriented Programming (OOP)" in JavaScript.

-Answer:Object-Oriented Programming is a programming paradigm that uses objects, which can contain data in the form of fields (attributes or properties) and code, in the form of procedures (methods or functions). In JavaScript, OOP features include classes, inheritance, encapsulation, and polymorphism.

```javascript
// OOP example with a class
class Animal {
    constructor(name) {
        this.name = name;
    }

    speak() {
        console.log(`${this.name} makes a sound.`);
    }
}

const cat = new Animal('Cat');
cat.speak(); // Output: 'Cat makes a sound.'
```

127.What is the purpose of the `String.prototype.replace()` method in JavaScript? Provide an example.

-Answer:The `replace()` method is used to replace a specified substring or pattern with another string. It does not modify the original string but returns a new one. Here's an example:

```javascript
const sentence = 'I love JavaScript!';
const newSentence = sentence.replace('JavaScript', 'React');

console.log(newSentence); // Output: 'I love React!'
```

128.Explain the concept of "Virtual DOM" in the context of JavaScript frameworks like React.

-Answer:The Virtual DOM is a concept used by JavaScript frameworks like React to improve performance in updating the actual DOM. Instead of directly manipulating the real DOM, changes are first made to a virtual representation of the DOM. The framework then calculates the most efficient way to update the actual DOM and applies the changes, reducing the number of direct DOM manipulations and enhancing application speed.

129.What is the purpose of the `Array.prototype.filter()` method in JavaScript? Provide an example.

-Answer:The `filter()` method is used to create a new array with elements that pass a provided testing function. It does not modify the original array. Here's an example:

```javascript
const numbers = [1, 2, 3, 4, 5];
const evenNumbers = numbers.filter(num => num % 2 === 0);

console.log(evenNumbers); // Output: [2, 4]
```

130.Explain the concept of "Debouncing" in JavaScript and how it can be implemented.

-Answer:Debouncing is a technique used to ensure that time-consuming tasks do not fire so often, making them more efficient. It involves delaying the execution of a function until after a certain amount of time has passed since the last invocation. This is useful for scenarios like handling user input, where you want to wait for a pause in typing before triggering an action. Debouncing can be implemented using `setTimeout` and `clearTimeout`.

```javascript
function debounce(func, delay) {
    let timeoutId;
```

131.What is the purpose of the `Array.prototype.every()` method in JavaScript? Provide an example.

Answer: The `every()` method is used to test whether all elements in an array pass a provided testing function. It returns `true` if all elements pass the test; otherwise, it returns `false`. Here's an example:

```javascript
const numbers = [2, 4, 6, 8, 10];
const allEven = numbers.every(num => num % 2 === 0);

console.log(allEven); // Output: true (because all elements are even)
```

132.Explain the concept of "Memoization" in JavaScript and how it can be implemented.

Answer: Memoization is an optimization technique that involves caching the results of expensive function calls and returning the cached result when the same inputs occur again. It helps improve the performance of functions by avoiding redundant computations. Memoization can be implemented using a cache object to store previously computed results.

```javascript
function memoize(fn) {
    const cache = {};

    return function(...args) {
        const key = JSON.stringify(args);
        if (cache[key] === undefined) {
            cache[key] = fn(...args);
        }
        return cache[key];
    };
}

const expensiveOperation = memoize(function(n) {
    console.log('Performing expensive operation...');
    return n * n;
});

console.log(expensiveOperation(5)); // Output: Performing expensive operation... 25
console.log(expensiveOperation(5)); // Output: 25 (cached result)
```

133.What is the purpose of the `Array.prototype.reduce()` method in JavaScript?
Provide an example.

Answer: The `reduce()` method is used to reduce an array to a single value by
applying a provided function to each element and accumulating the results. It takes an
accumulator and the current element as arguments and returns the accumulated
result. Here's an example:

```javascript
const numbers = [1, 2, 3, 4, 5];
const sum = numbers.reduce((acc, num) => acc + num, 0);

console.log(sum); // Output: 15 (1 + 2 + 3 + 4 + 5)
```

134.Explain the concept of "Hoisting" in JavaScript.

Answer: Hoisting is a JavaScript behavior where variable and function declarations
are moved to the top of their containing scope during the compilation phase. This
allows you to use a variable or function before it's declared in the code. However, only
the declarations are hoisted, not the initializations or assignments.

```javascript
console.log(x); // Output: undefined
var x = 5;
```

The code above is interpreted as if it were:

```javascript
var x;
console.log(x); // Output: undefined
x = 5;
```

135.What is the purpose of the `Array.prototype.forEach()` method in JavaScript? Provide an example.

Answer: The `forEach()` method is used to execute a provided function once for each array element. It does not return a new array but is often used for side effects or performing an action on each element. Here's an example:

```javascript
const colors = ['red', 'green', 'blue'];

colors.forEach((color, index) => {
    console.log(`Color at index ${index}: ${color}`);
});
```

136.Explain the concept of "Event Delegation" in JavaScript.

Answer: Event Delegation is a pattern where a single event listener is attached to a common ancestor of multiple elements. Instead of attaching an event listener to each individual element, the ancestor handles the events, and the event object's properties are used to identify the target element. This pattern is useful for efficiency, especially when dealing with a large number of dynamically created elements.

137. What is the purpose of the `String.prototype.substring()` method in JavaScript? Provide an example.

Answer: The `substring()` method is used to extract characters from a string between two specified indices. It returns a new string containing the extracted characters. Here's an example:

```javascript
const str = 'Hello, World!';
const substr = str.substring(7, 12);

console.log(substr); // Output: 'World'
```

138. Explain the concept of "Cross-Site Scripting (XSS)" in the context of web security.

Answer: Cross-Site Scripting (XSS) is a security vulnerability where an attacker injects malicious scripts into web pages viewed by other users. This can occur when user input is not properly validated or sanitized before being displayed on a web page. XSS attacks can lead to the theft of sensitive information, session hijacking, or other malicious activities.

139. What is the purpose of the `Array.prototype.some()` method in JavaScript? Provide an example.

Answer: The `some()` method is used to test whether at least one element in an array satisfies the provided testing function. It returns `true` if any element passes the test; otherwise, it returns `false`. Here's

an example:

```javascript
const numbers = [1, 2, 3, 4, 5];
const hasEven = numbers.some(num => num % 2 === 0);

console.log(hasEven); // Output: true (because 2 is even)
```

140.Explain the concept of "WebSockets" in JavaScript and how they differ from traditional HTTP requests.

Answer: WebSockets provide a full-duplex communication channel over a single, long-lived connection. Unlike traditional HTTP requests, which are stateless and follow a request-response model, WebSockets allow real-time, bidirectional communication between clients and servers. WebSockets are particularly useful for applications that require low latency and frequent updates, such as chat applications and online gaming.

141.What is the purpose of the `String.prototype.trim()` method in JavaScript? Provide an example.

Answer: The `trim()` method is used to remove whitespace from both ends of a string. It does not modify the original string but returns a new string with leading and trailing whitespaces removed. Here's an example:

```javascript
const str = '   Hello, World!   ';
const trimmedStr = str.trim();

console.log(trimmedStr); // Output: 'Hello, World!'
```

142.What is the purpose of the `Object.freeze()` method in JavaScript? Provide an example.

Answer: The `Object.freeze()` method is used to freeze an object, making it immutable. Once an object is frozen, you cannot add, delete, or modify its properties. Attempts to make such changes will result in an error. Here's an example:

```javascript
const person = { name: 'Alice', age: 30 };
Object.freeze(person);


// Trying to modify a frozen object
person.age = 31; // This will not have any effect, and no error will be thrown


console.log(person); // Output: { name: 'Alice', age: 30 }
```

143.Explain the concept of "Shadow DOM" in the context of web development.

Answer: Shadow DOM (Document Object Model) is a web standard that allows encapsulation of a component's style and structure, preventing its styles from leaking into or being affected by the styles of the main document. It is often used in web components to create isolated and reusable components with encapsulated styles and behavior.

144.What is the purpose of the `Array.prototype.flat()` method in JavaScript? Provide an example.

Answer: The `flat()` method is used to flatten nested arrays by a specified depth. It creates a new array with all sub-array elements concatenated into it recursively up to the specified depth. Here's an example:

```javascript
const nestedArray = [1, [2, [3, [4]]]];
const flattenedArray = nestedArray.flat(2);


console.log(flattenedArray); // Output: [1, 2, 3, 4]
```

145.Explain the concept of "Tail Call Optimization" in JavaScript.

Answer: Tail Call Optimization (TCO) is an optimization technique where the JavaScript engine recognizes tail calls (function calls made at the end of another function) and eliminates the need for additional stack frames. This can help prevent stack overflow errors in recursive functions. However, as of my knowledge cutoff in January 2022, TCO is not universally supported in all JavaScript engines.

146.What is the purpose of the `Array.from()` method in JavaScript? Provide an example.

Answer: The `Array.from()` method is used to create a new array instance from an iterable object or array-like object. It allows you to convert objects that are not inherently arrays into arrays. Here's an example:

```
const iterableObject = 'Hello';
const charArray = Array.from(iterableObject);

console.log(charArray); // Output: ['H', 'e', 'l', 'l', 'o']
```

147.Explain the concept of "IIFE" (Immediately Invoked Function Expression) in JavaScript.

Answer: IIFE is a JavaScript design pattern where a function is defined and immediately invoked. It helps create a private scope for variables and avoid polluting the global scope. Here's an example:

```
(function() {
    // Private scope
    const x = 10;
    console.log(x); // Output: 10
})();
```

148.What is the purpose of the `String.prototype.concat()` method in JavaScript? Provide an example.

Answer: The `concat()` method is used to concatenate one or more strings and return a new string. It does not modify the original strings. Here's an example:

```javascript
const str1 = 'Hello';
const str2 = ' ';
const str3 = 'World';

const result = str1.concat(str2, str3);

console.log(result); // Output: 'Hello World'
```

149.Explain the concept of "Event Loop" in JavaScript and how it facilitates asynchronous operations.

Answer: The Event Loop is a fundamental part of the JavaScript concurrency model. It continuously checks the message queue for events or functions to execute. When the call stack is empty, the event loop takes the first message from the queue and pushes it onto the call stack for execution. This process enables asynchronous operations, such as handling callbacks, promises, and setTimeout.

150.What is the purpose of the `Array.prototype.includes()` method in JavaScript? Provide an example.

Answer: The `includes()` method is used to determine whether an array includes a specific element. It returns `true` if the element is found; otherwise, it returns `false`. Here's an example:

```javascript
const numbers = [1, 2, 3, 4, 5];
const includesThree = numbers.includes(3);

console.log(includesThree); // Output: true
```

jQuery

1.What is jQuery?

Explanation:jQuery is a fast, lightweight, and feature-rich JavaScript library. It simplifies tasks like DOM manipulation, event handling, animation, and AJAX calls, making it easier for developers to create interactive and dynamic web pages.

2.How do you include jQuery in a web page?

Explanation:You can include jQuery in a web page by adding the following script tag in the HTML head or body section:

```html
<script src="https://code.jquery.com/jquery-3.6.4.min.js"></script>
```

3.Explain the difference between `$(document).ready()` and `$(window).load()` in jQuery.

Explanation:`$(document).ready()` is triggered when the DOM is fully loaded, while `$(window).load()` waits for all the content, including images, to be loaded. `$(document).ready()` is generally preferred for faster execution.

4.What is the significance of the dollar sign (`$`) in jQuery?

Explanation:The dollar sign is a shorthand alias for the `jQuery` object. It is used to reference jQuery methods and properties. For example, `$(selector)` is equivalent to `jQuery(selector)`.

5.Explain event delegation in jQuery.

Explanation:Event delegation involves attaching a single event listener to a common ancestor rather than individual elements. This allows you to handle events for dynamically added elements and improves performance. jQuery's `on()` method is commonly used for event delegation.

6.Differentiate between `$(this)` and `this` in jQuery.

Explanation:`$(this)` refers to the jQuery object representing the current DOM element, while `this` refers to the actual DOM element. When using jQuery methods, `$(this)` allows you to access jQuery functions, while `this` provides direct access to DOM properties and methods.

7.Explain the concept of chaining in jQuery.

Explanation:Chaining in jQuery allows you to execute multiple methods on the same set of elements in a single line. It enhances code readability and reduces the number of lines needed. For example:

```
$('#myElement').css('color', 'red').slideUp(2000).fadeIn(1000);
```

8.What is the purpose of the `noConflict()` method in jQuery?

Explanation:The `noConflict()` method is used to relinquish control of the `$` variable to other JavaScript libraries that might also use it. This is useful when there is a potential conflict between jQuery and another library.

9.Explain the difference between `append()` and `appendTo()` in jQuery.

Explanation:Both methods are used to insert content, but `append()` inserts content at the end of the selected element, while `appendTo()` inserts content at the end of the specified target element. The syntax differences are:

```
// append()
$(target).append(content);


// appendTo()
$(content).appendTo(target);
```

10.How does the `fadeOut()` function work in jQuery, and what is its purpose?

 Explanation:The `fadeOut()` function is used to gradually reduce the opacity of selected elements, causing them to fade out. It takes a duration parameter to specify the animation speed. For example:

```
$('#myElement').fadeOut(1000);
```

This code fades out the element with the ID 'myElement' over a period of 1000 milliseconds (1 second).

11.Explain the purpose of the `slideDown()` function in jQuery.

Explanation:The `slideDown()` function is used to display hidden elements with a sliding motion. It gradually increases the height of the selected elements, making them visible. It is often used in conjunction with `slideUp()` for hiding elements.

12.What is event propagation in jQuery, and how is it managed?

Explanation:Event propagation in jQuery refers to the flow of events through the DOM hierarchy. It can be categorized as capturing phase and bubbling phase. jQuery provides the `event.stopPropagation()` method to stop the event from propagating up or down the DOM tree, depending on the phase.

13.How does the `toggleClass()` function work in jQuery?

Explanation:The `toggleClass()` function is used to add or remove one or more classes from selected elements. If a class is present, it is removed, and if it is absent, it is added. This method simplifies toggling the visibility or styling of elements based on user actions.

14.Explain the difference between `attr()` and `prop()` in jQuery.

Explanation:The `attr()` method is used to get or set the value of HTML attributes, while the `prop()` method is used to get or set the value of properties. Attributes are typically defined in the HTML markup, while properties are dynamic values associated with DOM elements.

15.What is the purpose of the `$.ajax()` function in jQuery?

Explanation:The `$.ajax()` function is used for asynchronous HTTP requests, commonly known as AJAX (Asynchronous JavaScript and XML) calls. It allows you to send and receive data from a server without refreshing the entire page, enabling dynamic and responsive web applications.

16.How does the `animate()` function work in jQuery, and what are its parameters?

Explanation:The `animate()` function is used for creating custom animations on selected elements. It takes multiple parameters, such as properties to animate, duration, easing function, and a callback function. For example:

```
$('#myElement').animate({ left: '250px', opacity: 0.5 }, 1000, 'swing', function()
    // Animation complete callback
});
```

17.Explain the purpose of the `each()` function in jQuery.

Explanation:The `each()` function is used to iterate over a set of elements, executing a callback function for each element. It simplifies working with collections of elements, such as iterating through a list of items and performing an action on each one.

18.What is the significance of the `serialize()` method in jQuery?

Explanation:The `serialize()` method is used to create a URL-encoded string representation of form data. It is commonly used when sending form data via AJAX requests. This method simplifies the process of serializing form input values into a format that can be sent to the server.

19.How does the `empty()` function work in jQuery?

Explanation:The `empty()` function is used to remove all child elements and content from the selected elements. It essentially clears the HTML content inside the specified elements, making them empty.

20.Explain the purpose of the `$.getScript()` function in jQuery.

Explanation:The `$.getScript()` function is a shorthand method for making an AJAX request to load and execute an external JavaScript file. It simplifies the process of dynamically loading scripts into a web page, often used for loading scripts on demand.

21.What is event delegation in jQuery, and why is it beneficial?

Explanation: Event delegation in jQuery involves attaching a single event listener to a common ancestor instead of attaching multiple listeners to individual elements. This is beneficial for dynamically created elements as well as for performance optimization, as it reduces the number of event handlers.

22.Explain the purpose of the `slideUp()` function in jQuery.

Explanation: The `slideUp()` function is used to hide selected elements with a sliding motion. It gradually reduces the height of the elements, making them disappear. It is often used alongside `slideDown()` for creating toggle effects.

23.How does the `on()` method differ from `bind()` and `live()` in jQuery?

Explanation: While `bind()` and `live()` are older methods, `on()` is a more versatile and preferred method for event handling in jQuery. `on()` can handle current and future elements and provides a cleaner syntax for event binding.

24.What is the purpose of the `delay()` method in jQuery animations?

Explanation: The `delay()` method is used to introduce a delay or pause in the execution of animations in jQuery. It is often used in conjunction with other animation methods to create a pause between different animation steps.

25.Explain the difference between the `prepend()` and `prependTo()` methods in jQuery.

Explanation: Both methods are used to insert content, but `prepend()` inserts content at the beginning of the selected element, while `prependTo()` inserts content at the beginning of the specified target element. The syntax differences are similar to those of `append()` and `appendTo()`.

26.How does event bubbling work, and how can it be controlled in jQuery?

Explanation: Event bubbling is the process by which an event propagates from the target element to its ancestors in the DOM hierarchy. In jQuery, you can use `event.stopPropagation()` to stop the event from bubbling up the DOM tree, controlling the flow of the event.

27.Explain the purpose of the `serializeArray()` method in jQuery.

Explanation: The `serializeArray()` method is used to create an array of objects representing form field names and values. This is particularly useful when working with forms and sending the data to the server, as it provides a structured format for form data.

28.What is the role of the `is()` method in jQuery?

Explanation: The `is()` method is used to check whether selected elements match a specified selector, element, or jQuery object. It returns `true` if at least one of the selected elements matches the criteria and `false` otherwise. It is commonly used in conditional statements.

29.How can you handle AJAX errors in jQuery?

Explanation: jQuery provides the `error` callback function for handling errors in AJAX requests. This function is invoked when the request encounters an error, allowing developers to take appropriate actions, such as displaying an error message or logging the error.

30.Explain the purpose of the `fadeToggle()` function in jQuery.

Explanation: The `fadeToggle()` function is used to toggle the visibility of selected elements with a fading effect. If the elements are visible, the function fades them out; if they are hidden, it fades them in. It is a convenient method for creating toggle effects with a fading transition.

31.What is the purpose of the `wrap()` method in jQuery?

Explanation:The `wrap()` method is used to wrap an HTML structure around each element in the set of matched elements. It is useful for adding container elements around existing elements to change their structure or styling.

32.Explain the concept of method chaining in jQuery.

Explanation:Method chaining in jQuery involves calling multiple methods on a set of elements in a single statement. Each method returns a jQuery object, allowing you to chain additional methods together. This improves code readability and conciseness.

33.How can you make a cross-domain AJAX request in jQuery?

Explanation:Cross-domain AJAX requests are subject to the Same-Origin Policy. To overcome this restriction, you can use JSONP (JSON with Padding) or enable Cross-Origin Resource Sharing (CORS). jQuery's `$.ajax()` method supports these scenarios through the `dataType` option and appropriate server-side configurations.

34.What is the purpose of the `removeAttr()` method in jQuery?

Explanation:The `removeAttr()` method is used to remove specified attributes from the set of matched elements. It allows you to dynamically modify the attributes of HTML elements by removing existing ones.

35.Explain the role of the `slideDown()` and `slideUp()` functions in jQuery animations.

Explanation:`slideDown()` is used to reveal or show selected elements with a sliding motion by increasing their height. Conversely, `slideUp()` is used to hide elements with a sliding motion by reducing their height. These functions are commonly employed for toggle effects.

36.What is the purpose of the `clone()` method in jQuery?

Explanation:The `clone()` method is used to create a deep copy of the set of matched elements, including their descendants and properties. This allows you to duplicate elements in the DOM and manipulate the copies independently of the originals.

37.Explain the use of the `stop()` method in jQuery animations.

Explanation:The `stop()` method is used to stop animations in progress on the selected elements. It can be used to halt an ongoing animation or clear the animation queue. The method takes optional parameters to control whether to clear the queue or jump to the end of the animation.

38.What is the purpose of the `slideDown()` and `slideUp()` functions in jQuery animations?

Explanation:`slideDown()` is used to reveal or show selected elements with a sliding motion by increasing their height. Conversely, `slideUp()` is used to hide elements with a sliding motion by reducing their height. These functions are commonly employed for toggle effects.

39.Explain the concept of Deferred objects in jQuery.

Explanation:Deferred objects in jQuery are a mechanism for handling asynchronous operations. They represent a way to attach multiple callbacks to deferred tasks, such as AJAX requests, and manage their success or failure. Deferred objects are returned by methods like `$.ajax()`.

40.What is the purpose of the `wrapAll()` method in jQuery?

Explanation:The `wrapAll()` method is used to wrap a single container around all elements in a set of matched elements. It is similar to `wrap()`, but it wraps all the elements as a group rather than individually. This is useful for restructuring the HTML layout.

41.Explain the purpose of the `serialize()` method in jQuery.

Explanation: The `serialize()` method is used to create a URL-encoded string by serializing form values. It is commonly used to prepare data for AJAX requests when submitting forms. The resulting string can be sent to the server to process form data.

42.What is the purpose of the `toggleClass()` method in jQuery?

Explanation: The `toggleClass()` method is used to add or remove one or more classes from the selected elements. If a class is present, it is removed, and if it is absent, it is added. This method is particularly useful for toggling CSS styles based on user interactions.

43.Explain the difference between the `find()` and `filter()` methods in jQuery.

Explanation: The `find()` method is used to search for descendants of the selected elements, whereas the `filter()` method is used to narrow down the set of matched elements based on a specified criteria. `find()` looks for descendants at any level, while `filter()` operates on the current set of elements.

44.What is the purpose of the `slideDown()` and `slideUp()` functions in jQuery animations?

Explanation: `slideDown()` is used to reveal or show selected elements with a sliding motion by increasing their height. Conversely, `slideUp()` is used to hide elements with a sliding motion by reducing their height. These functions are commonly employed for toggle effects.

45.Explain the role of the `val()` method in jQuery.

Explanation: The `val()` method is used to get or set the value of form elements, such as input, select, and textarea elements. When used without parameters, it retrieves the current value, and when used with a parameter, it sets the value of the form element.

46.How does the `not()` method work in jQuery, and what is its purpose?

Explanation: The `not()` method is used to exclude elements from the set of matched elements based on a specified condition. It is helpful for filtering out elements that do not meet certain criteria, allowing you to work with a refined set of elements.

47.Explain the concept of method chaining in jQuery.

Explanation: Method chaining in jQuery involves calling multiple methods on a set of elements in a single statement. Each method returns a jQuery object, allowing you to chain additional methods together. This enhances code readability and reduces the need for intermediate variables.

48.What is the purpose of the `unwrap()` method in jQuery?

Explanation: The `unwrap()` method is used to remove the parent element of each set of matched elements. It essentially "unwraps" the selected elements from their containing parent, leaving them in the DOM without the former parent.

49.How can you check if an element is visible or hidden using jQuery?

Explanation: The `:visible` and `:hidden` selectors in jQuery allow you to check the visibility status of elements. For example:

```javascript
if ($('#myElement').is(':visible')) {
    // Element is visible
} else {
    // Element is hidden
}
```

50.What is the purpose of the `replaceWith()` method in jQuery?

Explanation: The `replaceWith()` method is used to replace each element in the set of matched elements with the specified HTML or DOM elements. It is useful for dynamically changing the content or structure of elements in the DOM.

51.Explain the purpose of the `$.getJSON()` function in jQuery.

Explanation:The `$.getJSON()` function is a shorthand method for making AJAX requests specifically designed for fetching JSON data. It simplifies the process of making asynchronous requests to a server and handling the JSON response.

52.What is the purpose of the `unwrap()` method in jQuery?

Explanation:The `unwrap()` method is used to remove the parent element of each set of matched elements. It essentially "unwraps" the selected elements from their containing parent, leaving them in the DOM without the former parent.

53.Explain the difference between the `html()` and `text()` methods in jQuery.

Explanation:The `html()` method is used to get or set the HTML content of elements, including any HTML tags. On the other hand, the `text()` method retrieves or sets the text content of elements, stripping out any HTML tags. Use `html()` when dealing with HTML content and `text()` for plain text.

54.How can you create an element and append it to the DOM using jQuery?

Explanation:You can use the `$(html)` syntax to create a new element, and then use various methods like `append()`, `appendTo()`, `prepend()`, or `prependTo()` to insert it into the DOM. For example:

```
$('<div>New Element</div>').appendTo('#container');
```

55.Explain the purpose of the `slideUp()` and `slideDown()` functions in jQuery animations.

Explanation:`slideUp()` is used to hide selected elements with a sliding motion by reducing their height, while `slideDown()` is used to reveal or show elements with a sliding motion by increasing their height. These functions are commonly used to create animated toggle effects.

56.What is the role of the `slideToggle()` function in jQuery?

Explanation:The `slideToggle()` function is used to toggle the visibility of selected elements with a sliding motion. If the elements are visible, it hides them with a sliding motion; if they are hidden, it shows them. This function is convenient for creating toggle effects with a sliding animation.

57.Explain the purpose of the `closest()` method in jQuery.

Explanation:The `closest()` method is used to find the closest ancestor of the selected elements that matches a given selector. It traverses up the DOM tree, starting from the current element, until it finds the first element that matches the specified selector.

58.How can you dynamically add and remove classes in jQuery?

Explanation:You can use the `addClass()` method to add one or more classes to the selected elements and the `removeClass()` method to remove classes. Additionally, `toggleClass()` can be used to toggle the presence of a class based on its current state.

59.Explain the purpose of the `slideDown()` and `slideUp()` functions in jQuery animations.

Explanation:`slideUp()` is used to hide selected elements with a sliding motion by reducing their height, while `slideDown()` is used to reveal or show elements with a sliding motion by increasing their height. These functions are commonly used to create animated toggle effects.

60.What is the purpose of the `offset()` method in jQuery?

Explanation:The `offset()` method is used to get the current coordinates of the first element in the set of matched elements, relative to the document. It returns an object with `top` and `left` properties representing the element's position. This can be useful for positioning elements dynamically.

61.What is event delegation in jQuery, and why is it beneficial?

Explanation:Event delegation in jQuery involves attaching a single event listener to a common ancestor instead of attaching multiple listeners to individual elements. This is beneficial for dynamically created elements as well as for performance optimization, as it reduces the number of event handlers.

62.How can you prevent the default behavior of an event in jQuery?

Explanation:To prevent the default behavior of an event, you can use the `event.preventDefault()` method. This is often used within event handler functions to stop the default action associated with a particular event, such as preventing the submission of a form or the opening of a link.

63.Explain the purpose of the `unwrap()` method in jQuery.

Explanation:The `unwrap()` method is used to remove the parent element of each set of matched elements. It essentially "unwraps" the selected elements from their containing parent, leaving them in the DOM without the former parent.

64.How does the `one()` method differ from the `on()` method in jQuery?

Explanation:The `one()` method is similar to `on()`, but it attaches an event handler that will only be executed once. After the event is triggered and the handler is executed, it is automatically removed. This is useful for handling events that should only occur once.

65.What is the purpose of the `empty()` method in jQuery?

Explanation:The `empty()` method is used to remove all child elements and content from the selected elements. It effectively clears the HTML content inside the specified elements, making them empty.

66.Explain the use of the `fadeTo()` method in jQuery.

Explanation:The `fadeTo()` method is used to adjust the opacity of selected elements to a specified level. It takes two parameters: the duration of the fade and the target opacity. This method is useful for creating smooth transitions in the visibility of elements.

67.How does the `slideDown()` function work in jQuery, and what is its purpose?

Explanation:The `slideDown()` function is used to display hidden elements with a sliding motion. It gradually increases the height of the selected elements, making them visible. It is often used in conjunction with `slideUp()` for hiding elements.

68.Explain the purpose of the `serializeArray()` method in jQuery.

Explanation:The `serializeArray()` method is used to create an array of objects representing form field names and values. This is particularly useful when working with forms and sending the data to the server, as it provides a structured format for form data.

69.What is the purpose of the `replaceWith()` method in jQuery?

Explanation:The `replaceWith()` method is used to replace each element in the set of matched elements with the specified HTML or DOM elements. It is useful for dynamically changing the content or structure of elements in the DOM.

70.Explain the concept of event propagation in jQuery.

Explanation:Event propagation in jQuery refers to the order in which events are handled as they travel through the DOM hierarchy. It includes the capturing phase and the bubbling phase. The `event.stopPropagation()` method can be used to stop the event from propagating further.

71.What is the purpose of the `replaceWith()` method in jQuery?

Explanation: The `replaceWith()` method is used to replace each element in the set of matched elements with the specified HTML or DOM elements. It is useful for dynamically changing the content or structure of elements in the DOM.

72.How does the `hasClass()` method work in jQuery, and what is its purpose?

Explanation: The `hasClass()` method is used to check whether any of the selected elements have a specified class. It returns `true` if at least one element has the class and `false` otherwise. This method is useful for conditional logic based on the presence of a class.

73.Explain the concept of event propagation in jQuery.

Explanation: Event propagation in jQuery refers to the order in which events are handled as they travel through the DOM hierarchy. It includes the capturing phase and the bubbling phase. The `event.stopPropagation()` method can be used to stop the event from propagating further.

74.What is the purpose of the `prepend()` method in jQuery?

Explanation: The `prepend()` method is used to insert content, specified by the parameter, at the beginning of each element in the set of matched elements. It is similar to `append()`, but it inserts content at the beginning rather than the end.

75.How does the `parent()` method work in jQuery, and what is its purpose?

Explanation: The `parent()` method is used to get the direct parent of each element in the set of matched elements. It traverses up the DOM tree and returns the immediate parent element. This is useful for navigating the DOM hierarchy.

76.Explain the purpose of the `siblings()` method in jQuery.

Explanation: The `siblings()` method is used to get the siblings of each element in the set of matched elements. It returns a set of elements that share the same parent with the original set. This method is useful for selecting elements that are at the same level in the DOM hierarchy.

77.How can you create a custom animation using the `animate()` method in jQuery?

Explanation: The `animate()` method in jQuery allows you to create custom animations by specifying a set of CSS properties and values to animate. You can define the target properties, duration, easing function, and a callback function to be executed when the animation is complete.

78.What is the purpose of the `toggleClass()` method in jQuery?

Explanation: The `toggleClass()` method is used to add or remove one or more classes from the selected elements. If a class is present, it is removed; if it is absent, it is added. This method is particularly useful for toggling styles based on user interactions.

79.How can you make an AJAX request using the `$.ajax()` method in jQuery?

Explanation: The `$.ajax()` method is used for making AJAX requests in jQuery. You can specify various options, such as the URL, type of request (GET or POST), data to be sent, success and error callbacks, etc. This method provides a flexible way to handle asynchronous communication with the server.

80.Explain the purpose of the `slideDown()` and `slideUp()` functions in jQuery animations.

Explanation: `slideDown()` is used to reveal or show selected elements with a sliding motion by increasing their height, while `slideUp()` is used to hide elements with a sliding motion by reducing their height. These functions are commonly used to create animated toggle effects.

81.What is the purpose of the `unwrap()` method in jQuery?

Explanation: The `unwrap()` method is used to remove the parent element of each set of matched elements. It essentially "unwraps" the selected elements from their containing parent, leaving them in the DOM without the former parent.

82.How does the `serialize()` method work in jQuery, and when is it commonly used?

Explanation: The `serialize()` method is used to create a URL-encoded string representation of form data. It is commonly used when sending form data via AJAX requests. This method serializes the form input values into a format that can be easily sent to the server for processing.

83.What is the purpose of the `replaceWith()` method in jQuery?

Explanation: The `replaceWith()` method is used to replace each element in the set of matched elements with the specified HTML or DOM elements. It is useful for dynamically changing the content or structure of elements in the DOM.

84.How does the `slideDown()` function work in jQuery, and what is its purpose?

Explanation: The `slideDown()` function is used to display hidden elements with a sliding motion. It gradually increases the height of the selected elements, making them visible. It is often used in conjunction with `slideUp()` for hiding elements.

85.Explain the concept of method chaining in jQuery.

Explanation: Method chaining in jQuery involves calling multiple methods on a set of elements in a single statement. Each method returns a jQuery object, allowing you to chain additional methods together. This enhances code readability and conciseness.

86.What is the purpose of the `promise()` method in jQuery?

Explanation: The `promise()` method is used to return a Promise object that represents the state of a set of deferred objects. It is often used in conjunction with animations and AJAX requests to perform actions based on the completion or failure of these asynchronous operations.

87.Explain the purpose of the `fadeToggle()` function in jQuery.

Explanation: The `fadeToggle()` function is used to toggle the visibility of selected elements with a fading effect. If the elements are visible, it fades them out; if they are hidden, it fades them in. This function is a convenient method for creating toggle effects with a fading transition.

88.How can you delay the execution of code in jQuery?

Explanation: The `setTimeout()` function can be used to introduce a delay in the execution of code. It takes a callback function and a specified delay time in milliseconds. This is often used to create delayed animations or to perform actions after a certain period.

89.What is the purpose of the `text()` method in jQuery?

Explanation: The `text()` method is used to get or set the text content of elements. It retrieves the combined text content of all matched elements or sets the text content to the specified value. This method is commonly used for manipulating text within HTML elements.

90.Explain the purpose of the `fadeTo()` method in jQuery.

Explanation: The `fadeTo()` method is used to adjust the opacity of selected elements to a specified level. It takes two parameters: the duration of the fade and the target opacity. This method is useful for creating smooth transitions in the visibility of elements.

91.What is the purpose of the `unwrap()` method in jQuery?

Explanation: The `unwrap()` method is used to remove the parent element of each set of matched elements. It essentially "unwraps" the selected elements from their containing parent, leaving them in the DOM without the former parent.

92.How does event delegation work, and why is it beneficial in jQuery?

Explanation: Event delegation in jQuery involves attaching a single event listener to a common ancestor instead of attaching multiple listeners to individual elements. This is beneficial for dynamically created elements and improves performance by reducing the number of event handlers.

93.Explain the purpose of the `wrap()` method in jQuery.

Explanation: The `wrap()` method is used to wrap an HTML structure around each element in the set of matched elements. It allows you to add container elements around existing elements, which can be useful for styling or layout purposes.

94.What is the purpose of the `filter()` method in jQuery?

Explanation: The `filter()` method is used to narrow down the set of matched elements based on a specified criteria. It allows you to filter elements that meet certain conditions, providing a more refined selection.

95.How can you check if an element has a specific attribute using jQuery?

Explanation: The `attr()` method can be used to check if an element has a specific attribute. If the attribute exists, the method returns the attribute value; otherwise, it returns `undefined`. This can be used in conditional statements to check for the presence of an attribute.

96.Explain the purpose of the `slideToggle()` method in jQuery.

Explanation: The `slideToggle()` method is used to toggle the visibility of selected elements with a sliding motion. If the elements are visible, it hides them with a sliding motion; if they are hidden, it shows them. This method is convenient for creating toggle effects with a sliding animation.

97.How does the `delay()` method work in jQuery animations?

Explanation: The `delay()` method is used to introduce a delay or pause in the execution of animations in jQuery. It can be applied to animation methods, specifying the delay time in milliseconds before the animation begins.

98.Explain the concept of Deferred objects in jQuery.

Explanation: Deferred objects in jQuery represent the state of asynchronous operations. They provide a way to attach multiple callbacks to tasks such as AJAX requests and manage their success or failure. Deferred objects are returned by methods like `$.ajax()`.

99.What is the purpose of the `empty()` method in jQuery?

Explanation: The `empty()` method is used to remove all child elements and content from the selected elements. It essentially clears the HTML content inside the specified elements, making them empty.

100.How does the `closest()` method work in jQuery, and when is it commonly used?

Explanation: The `closest()` method is used to find the closest ancestor of the selected elements that matches a given selector. It traverses up the DOM tree, starting from the current element, until it finds the first element that matches the specified selector. This method is commonly used for navigation and DOM traversal.

101.What is the purpose of the `prev()` and `next()` methods in jQuery?

Explanation: The `prev()` method is used to get the immediately preceding sibling of each element in the set of matched elements. Conversely, the `next()` method gets the immediately following sibling. These methods are helpful for navigating through sibling elements in the DOM.

102.Explain the role of the `slideDown()` and `slideUp()` functions in jQuery animations.

Explanation: `slideDown()` is used to reveal or show selected elements with a sliding motion by increasing their height, while `slideUp()` is used to hide elements with a sliding motion by reducing their height. These functions are commonly used to create animated toggle effects.

103.What is the purpose of the `replaceWith()` method in jQuery?

Explanation: The `replaceWith()` method is used to replace each element in the set of matched elements with the specified HTML or DOM elements. It is useful for dynamically changing the content or structure of elements in the DOM.

104.Explain the use of the `serializeArray()` method in jQuery.

Explanation: The `serializeArray()` method is used to create an array of objects representing form field names and values. This is particularly useful when working with forms and sending the data to the server, as it provides a structured format for form data.

105.How can you dynamically add and remove classes in jQuery?

Explanation: You can use the `addClass()` method to add one or more classes to the selected elements and the `removeClass()` method to remove classes. Additionally, `toggleClass()` can be used to toggle the presence of a class based on its current state.

106.Explain the purpose of the `animate()` function in jQuery, and what parameters does it accept?

Explanation: The `animate()` function is used for creating custom animations on selected elements. It accepts parameters such as properties to animate, duration, easing function, and a callback function. For example:

```javascript
$('#myElement').animate({ left: '250px', opacity: 0.5 }, 1000, 'swing', function() {
    // Animation complete callback
});
```

107.What is the purpose of the `context` parameter in jQuery AJAX requests?

Explanation: The `context` parameter in jQuery AJAX requests allows you to set the value of `this` within the callback functions. It specifies the object to which the callbacks are bound. This can be useful for maintaining a specific context when working with asynchronous operations.

108.Explain the difference between `detach()` and `remove()` in jQuery.

Explanation: Both `detach()` and `remove()` are used to remove elements from the DOM. The key difference is that `detach()` also keeps the data and events associated with the removed elements, allowing them to be reinserted later, while `remove()` permanently removes the elements along with their data and events.

109.How can you handle AJAX errors in jQuery?

Explanation: jQuery provides the `error` callback function for handling errors in AJAX requests. This function is invoked when the request encounters an error, allowing developers to take appropriate actions, such as displaying an error message or logging the error.

110.What is the purpose of the `slideUp()` and `slideDown()` functions in jQuery animations?

Explanation: `slideUp()` is used to hide selected elements with a sliding motion by reducing their height, while `slideDown()` is used to reveal or show elements with a sliding motion by increasing their height. These functions are commonly used to create animated toggle effects.

111.What is the purpose of the `wrapAll()` method in jQuery?

Explanation: The `wrapAll()` method is used to wrap a single container around all elements in a set of matched elements. It is similar to `wrap()`, but it wraps all the elements as a group rather than individually. This is useful for restructuring the HTML layout.

112.Explain the use of the `prop()` method in jQuery.

Explanation: The `prop()` method is used to get or set properties of elements, such as checkboxes or radio buttons. It is an alternative to the `attr()` method when dealing with boolean attributes like "checked" or "disabled". The `prop()` method should be used for properties, and `attr()` for attributes.

113.What is the purpose of the `serialize()` method in jQuery?

Explanation: The `serialize()` method is used to create a URL-encoded string by serializing form values. It is commonly used to prepare data for AJAX requests when submitting forms. The resulting string can be sent to the server to process form data.

114.Explain the role of the `fadeOut()` and `fadeIn()` functions in jQuery animations.

Explanation: `fadeOut()` is used to gradually hide selected elements by reducing their opacity, while `fadeIn()` is used to reveal or show elements by increasing their opacity. These functions are commonly used for creating smooth fading effects.

115.How does the `wrapInner()` method work in jQuery?

Explanation: The `wrapInner()` method is used to wrap the content (including child elements) of each matched element with an HTML structure. It does not modify the element itself but wraps its contents. This is useful for applying styling or structural changes to the inner content.

116.What is the purpose of the `fadeIn()` and `fadeOut()` functions in jQuery animations?

Explanation: `fadeIn()` is used to gradually show selected elements by increasing their opacity, while `fadeOut()` is used to hide elements by reducing their opacity. These functions are commonly used for creating smooth fading effects.

117.Explain the concept of function queuing in jQuery animations.

Explanation: Function queuing in jQuery animations allows you to queue multiple functions to be executed on a set of elements in a sequential order. This is achieved using the `queue()` method. It is particularly useful when you want to create complex animations with multiple steps.

118.How does the `empty()` method differ from the `remove()` method in jQuery?

Explanation: The `empty()` method is used to remove all child elements and content from the selected elements, leaving the elements themselves intact. In contrast, the `remove()` method removes both the selected elements and their data, events, and descendants.

119.What is the purpose of the `slideToggle()` function in jQuery?

Explanation: The `slideToggle()` function is used to toggle the visibility of selected elements with a sliding motion. If the elements are visible, it hides them with a sliding motion; if they are hidden, it shows them. This function is convenient for creating toggle effects with a sliding animation.

120. Explain the use of the `closest()` method in jQuery.

Explanation: The `closest()` method is used to find the closest ancestor of the selected elements that matches a given selector. It traverses up the DOM tree, starting from the current element, until it finds the first element that matches the specified selector. This is useful for DOM traversal and navigation.

121. Explain the purpose of the `hasClass()` method in jQuery.

Explanation: The `hasClass()` method is used to check if any of the selected elements have a specified class. It returns `true` if at least one element has the class, and `false` otherwise. This method is commonly used for conditional logic based on the presence or absence of a class.

122. What is the purpose of the `unwrap()` method in jQuery?

Explanation: The `unwrap()` method is used to remove the parent element of each set of matched elements. It essentially "unwraps" the selected elements from their containing parent, leaving them in the DOM without the former parent.

123. How does event delegation work in jQuery, and why is it beneficial?

Explanation: Event delegation in jQuery involves attaching a single event listener to a common ancestor, rather than attaching multiple listeners to individual elements. This is beneficial for dynamically created elements and helps improve performance by reducing the number of event handlers.

124. Explain the purpose of the `prependTo()` method in jQuery.

Explanation: The `prependTo()` method is used to insert content, specified by the parameter, at the beginning of each element in the set of matched elements. It is similar to `prepend()`, but it reverses the order of the selection and target elements.

125. What is the purpose of the `siblings()` method in jQuery?

Explanation: The `siblings()` method is used to get the siblings of each element in the set of matched elements. It returns a set of elements that share the same parent with the original set. This method is useful for selecting elements that are at the same level in the DOM hierarchy.

126.Explain the use of the `not()` method in jQuery.

Explanation: The `not()` method is used to exclude elements from the set of matched elements based on a specified condition. It allows you to filter out elements that do not meet certain criteria, providing a more refined set of elements.

127.What is the purpose of the `context` parameter in jQuery AJAX requests?

Explanation: The `context` parameter in jQuery AJAX requests allows you to set the value of `this` within the callback functions. It specifies the object to which the callbacks are bound. This can be useful for maintaining a specific context when working with asynchronous operations.

128.Explain the role of the `toggle()` method in jQuery.

Explanation: The `toggle()` method is used to toggle between two or more functions or sets of elements. It alternates between the specified functions or elements on each click. This method is useful for creating toggle effects and switching between different states.

129.How can you create a fade-in effect on an element using jQuery?

Explanation: You can create a fade-in effect using the `fadeIn()` method. For example:

```
$('#myElement').fadeIn(1000); // Fades in over 1 second
```

130.What is the purpose of the `parentsUntil()` method in jQuery?

Explanation: The `parentsUntil()` method is used to get the ancestors of each element in the set of matched elements, up to but not including the element matched by the selector, DOM node, or jQuery object. It allows you to select a range of ancestor elements within the DOM hierarchy.

131.How does the `serialize()` method differ from `serializeArray()` in jQuery?

Explanation: Both `serialize()` and `serializeArray()` are used to create a serialized representation of form data. However, `serialize()` creates a URL-encoded string, suitable for AJAX requests, while `serializeArray()` creates an array of objects representing form field names and values.

132.Explain the purpose of the `before()` and `after()` methods in jQuery.

Explanation: The `before()` method is used to insert content or elements before each element in the set of matched elements, while `after()` is used to insert content or elements after each element in the set. These methods are helpful for manipulating the structure of the DOM.

133.What is the purpose of the `appendTo()` method in jQuery?

Explanation: The `appendTo()` method is used to insert content, specified by the parameter, to the end of each element in the set of matched elements. It is similar to `append()`, but it reverses the order of the selection and target elements.

134.How does the `children()` method work in jQuery, and when is it commonly used?

Explanation: The `children()` method is used to get the immediate children of each element in the set of matched elements. It returns a set of elements that are direct children of the selected elements. This method is commonly used for selecting and manipulating the children of a parent element.

135.Explain the purpose of the `not(':animated')` selector in jQuery animations.

Explanation: The `:animated` selector in jQuery is used to filter elements that are currently in the process of animation. When combined with `not(':animated')`, it selects elements that are not currently being animated. This is useful for preventing multiple animations from queuing up on the same element.

136.How can you handle cross-domain AJAX requests in jQuery?

Explanation: Cross-domain AJAX requests are subject to the same-origin policy. To handle them in jQuery, you can use JSONP (JSON with Padding) or CORS (Cross-Origin Resource Sharing). JSONP works by injecting a script tag with a callback function, while CORS involves server-side configuration and browser support.

137.What is the purpose of the `slideToggle()` method in jQuery?

Explanation: The `slideToggle()` method is used to toggle the visibility of selected elements with a sliding motion. If the elements are visible, it hides them with a sliding motion; if they are hidden, it shows them. This function is convenient for creating toggle effects with a sliding animation.

138.Explain the role of the `serialize()` method in jQuery AJAX requests.

Explanation: The `serialize()` method in jQuery is used to create a URL-encoded string representation of form data. When sending form data via an AJAX request, you can use this method to serialize the form values and include them in the data payload of the request.

139.How does the `fadeTo()` method differ from `fadeIn()` and `fadeOut()` in jQuery?

Explanation: The `fadeTo()` method is used to adjust the opacity of selected elements to a specified level, providing a more fine-grained control over the fading effect. In contrast, `fadeIn()` and `fadeOut()` are specifically designed for revealing and hiding elements by adjusting their opacity.

140.What is the purpose of the `is()` method in jQuery?

Explanation: The `is()` method is used to check the current set of matched elements against a selector, element, or jQuery object. It returns `true` if at least one element in the set matches the specified criteria and `false` otherwise. This method is useful for conditional checks in jQuery code.

141.What is event propagation, and how does it work in jQuery?

Explanation: Event propagation in jQuery refers to the order in which events are handled as they traverse the DOM hierarchy. It includes two phases: the capturing phase and the bubbling phase. The `event.stopPropagation()` method can be used to stop the event from propagating further in either phase.

142.Explain the purpose of the `empty()` method in jQuery.

Explanation: The `empty()` method is used to remove all child elements and content from the selected elements. It effectively clears the HTML content inside the specified elements, making them empty. This method is often used when you want to remove the content within an element without removing the element itself.

143. How can you prevent the default behavior of an event in jQuery?

Explanation: To prevent the default behavior of an event, you can use the `event.preventDefault()` method. This method is commonly used within event handler functions to stop the default action associated with a particular event, such as preventing the submission of a form or the opening of a link.

144. What is the purpose of the `fadeToggle()` method in jQuery?

Explanation: The `fadeToggle()` method is used to toggle the visibility of selected elements with a fading effect. If the elements are visible, it fades them out; if they are hidden, it fades them in. This method is a convenient way to create toggle effects with a smooth fading transition.

145. Explain the concept of method chaining in jQuery.

Explanation: Method chaining in jQuery involves calling multiple methods on a set of elements in a single statement. Each method returns a jQuery object, allowing you to chain additional methods together. This approach enhances code readability and conciseness.

146. What is the purpose of the `offset()` method in jQuery?

Explanation: The `offset()` method is used to get the current coordinates of the first element in the set of matched elements, relative to the document. It returns an object with `top` and `left` properties representing the element's position. This method is useful for determining the position of an element on the page.

147. Explain the purpose of the `slideDown()` function in jQuery animations.

Explanation: The `slideDown()` function is used to display hidden elements with a sliding motion. It gradually increases the height of the selected elements, making them visible. This function is often used in conjunction with `slideUp()` for hiding elements.

148. How does event delegation work in jQuery, and why is it beneficial?

Explanation: Event delegation in jQuery involves attaching a single event listener to a common ancestor, rather than attaching multiple listeners to individual elements. This is beneficial for dynamically created elements and improves performance by reducing the number of event handlers.

149.What is the purpose of the `removeAttr()` method in jQuery?

Explanation: The `removeAttr()` method is used to remove one or more attributes from the selected elements. It allows you to dynamically modify the attributes of elements in the DOM. This method is often used when you want to remove attributes like `disabled` or `readonly` from form elements.

150.How can you create a custom animation using the `animate()` method in jQuery?

Explanation: The `animate()` method in jQuery allows you to create custom animations by specifying a set of CSS properties and values to animate. You can define the target properties, duration, easing function, and a callback function to be executed when the animation is complete.

HTML

1.What is HTML?

Answer: HTML stands for HyperText Markup Language. It is the standard markup language used to create web pages. HTML is written in the form of tags, which are surrounded by angle brackets `< >`, to describe the structure of web documents.

2.Explain the basic structure of an HTML document.

Answer: An HTML document has a standard structure with the following elements:

```html
<!DOCTYPE html>
<html>
  <head>
    <title>Title of the Document</title>
  </head>
  <body>
    <!-- Content goes here -->
  </body>
</html>
```

`<!DOCTYPE html>`: Declaration of the HTML version.

  `<html>`: The root element of the HTML document.

  `<head>`: Contains meta-information about the HTML document.

  `<title>`: Sets the title of the document (shown in the browser tab).

  `<body>`: Contains the content of the HTML document.

3.What is the purpose of the `DOCTYPE` declaration?

Answer: The `DOCTYPE` declaration specifies the HTML version being used (e.g., HTML5). It helps browsers to render web pages correctly by providing information about the document type and version.

4.What is the difference between HTML and XHTML?

Answer: XHTML (Extensible Hypertext Markup Language) is a stricter, more XML-based version of HTML. The main differences include:

XHTML documents must be well-formed XML, meaning all tags must be properly nested and closed.

XHTML documents must have a DOCTYPE declaration.

XHTML attribute values must be enclosed in quotes.

5.Explain the purpose of HTML tags and attributes.

Answer: HTML tags are used to define elements on a web page, such as headings, paragraphs, links, etc. Attributes provide additional information about HTML elements and are always included in the opening tag. For example:

```html
<a href="https://www.example.com">Visit Example</a>
```

 In this example, `<a>` is the tag, and `href` is an attribute that specifies the link's destination.

6.What is the difference between `<div>` and `<span>` elements?

Answer: `<div>` and `<span>` are both container elements, but `<div>` is a block-level element used to group larger sections of content, while `<span>` is an inline element used to apply styles or manipulate small pieces of content within a larger block.

7.Explain the difference between the `<em>` and `<strong>` tags.

Answer: `<em>` is used to emphasize text, typically displayed in italics, while `<strong>` is used to indicate stronger importance, often displayed as bold text. Both elements are used to provide semantic meaning to the content.

8.What is the purpose of the `<meta>` tag?

Answer: The `<meta>` tag is used to provide metadata about the HTML document, such as character set, viewport settings, description, and keywords. For example:

```html
<meta charset="UTF-8">
<meta name="viewport" content="width=device-width, initial-scale=1.0">
```

9.Explain the difference between the `<ol>` and `<ul>` elements.

Answer: `<ol>` is used to create ordered lists (numbered lists), while `<ul>` is used to create unordered lists (bulleted lists). List items are represented by the `<li>` (list item) element.

10.What is the purpose of the `alt` attribute in the `<img>` tag?

Answer: The `alt` attribute in the `<img>` tag is used to provide alternative text for an image. This text is displayed if the image cannot be loaded or for accessibility purposes, helping users with screen readers understand the content of the image.

11.Explain the purpose of the `<iframe>` tag in HTML.

Answer: The `<iframe>` (Inline Frame) tag is used to embed another HTML document within the current document. It is often used to include external content, such as videos, maps, or other web pages, into a webpage.

12.What is the significance of the `colspan` and `rowspan` attributes in a table?

Answer: The `colspan` attribute is used to define the number of columns a table cell should span, while `rowspan` defines the number of rows. These attributes are commonly used to merge cells horizontally or vertically in a table.

13.Explain the purpose of the HTML `<form>` element.

Answer: The `<form>` element is used to create an HTML form that allows users to input data. It is often used to collect user information, and the form's content is typically sent to a server for processing using the `action` attribute.

14.What is the difference between the `<link>` tag and the `<a>` tag?

Answer: The `<link>` tag is used to link external resources, such as stylesheets or icons, to an HTML document. On the other hand, the `<a>` tag is an anchor tag used to create hyperlinks to navigate within the same document or to external pages.

15.Explain the purpose of the HTML5 `<canvas>` element.

Answer: The `<canvas>` element is used to draw graphics, charts, or other visual elements on a web page. JavaScript is commonly used to interact with the canvas and create dynamic and interactive visuals.

16.What is the purpose of the HTML5 `<article>` and `<section>` elements?

Answer: The `<article>` element is used to represent a self-contained piece of content, such as a blog post or news article. The `<section>` element, on the other hand, is used to group related content within an HTML document.

17.Explain the use of the `download` attribute in the `<a>` tag.

Answer: The `download` attribute in the `<a>` tag is used to specify that the target should be downloaded when a user clicks the link. It is often used for links to files, allowing users to download the file instead of navigating to it.

18.What is the purpose of the HTML `<aside>` element?

Answer: The `<aside>` element is used to define content that is tangentially related to the content around it. It is often used for sidebars, pull quotes, or other content that complements the main content but can be considered separate.

19.Explain the difference between the `GET` and `POST` methods in an HTML form.

Answer: The `GET` method is used to request data from a specified resource, and the data is appended to the URL. The `POST` method, on the other hand, is used to submit data to be processed to a specified resource, with the data included in the request body.

20.What is the purpose of the HTML `<progress>` element?

Answer: The `<progress>` element is used to represent the progress of a task. It can be used to show the completion percentage of a download, file upload, or any other task that involves a measurable progress.

21.What is the purpose of the `placeholder` attribute in an HTML `<input>` element?

Answer: The `placeholder` attribute is used to provide a short hint or example of the expected value in an input field. It is displayed in the input field before the user enters their own content.

22.Explain the role of the `hidden` attribute in HTML.

Answer: The `hidden` attribute is used to hide elements on a web page. When applied to an element, it will not be displayed in the browser. This can be useful for hiding or revealing content dynamically using JavaScript.

23.What is the purpose of the HTML `<nav>` element?

Answer: The `<nav>` element is used to define a set of navigation links on a web page. It is typically used to create navigation menus, lists of links, or other navigational elements.

24.Explain the difference between the `<b>` and `<strong>` tags in HTML.

Answer: Both `<b>` and `<strong>` are used to make text bold, but `<strong>` is a semantic element indicating strong importance, while `<b>` is a presentational element indicating bold text without implying strong importance.

25.How does the HTML5 `localStorage` differ from `sessionStorage`?

Answer: Both `localStorage` and `sessionStorage` are web storage objects that allow data to be stored on the client-side. The key difference is in their scope and lifetime. `localStorage` persists even when the browser is closed and has no expiration time, while `sessionStorage` is only available for the duration of the page session and is cleared when the session ends.

26.Explain the purpose of the `defer` attribute in the `<script>` tag.

Answer: The `defer` attribute in the `<script>` tag is used to indicate that the script should be executed after the HTML document has been fully parsed. This can improve page loading performance, especially when scripts are placed in the `<head>` section.

27.What is the purpose of the HTML `<abbr>` element?

Answer: The `<abbr>` element is used to define abbreviations or acronyms on a web page. It can include an optional `title` attribute that provides an expansion or explanation of the abbreviation when the user hovers over it.

28.Explain the purpose of the `async` attribute in the `<script>` tag.

Answer: The `async` attribute in the `<script>` tag is used to indicate that the script should be executed asynchronously, meaning it won't block the rendering of the page while the script is being downloaded. This is particularly useful for non-essential scripts.

29.What is the purpose of the HTML `<time>` element?

Answer: The `<time>` element is used to represent a specific period in time or a range of time on a web page. It can include a `datetime` attribute to provide machine-readable information about the time.

30.Explain the concept of semantic HTML.

Answer: Semantic HTML involves using HTML elements that carry meaning about the structure and content of a web page. It emphasizes using tags like `<header>`, `<nav>`, `<article>`, `<section>`, `<footer>`, etc., to convey the intended meaning of different parts of the document, making it more accessible and understandable for both developers and assistive technologies.

31.Explain the purpose of the `contenteditable` attribute in HTML.

Answer:The `contenteditable` attribute is used to make an element editable, allowing users to modify the content within that element directly. It is often used with `<div>` or `<span>` elements to create rich-text editors.

32.What is the purpose of the HTML `<details>` and `<summary>` elements?

Answer:The `<details>` element is used to create a disclosure widget from which the user can open or close additional information. The `<summary>` element is used as a summary or caption for the content within the `<details>` element.

33.Explain the difference between the `border` and `outline` CSS properties.

Answer:The `border` property is used to set the border of an element, defining its width, style, and color. The `outline` property, on the other hand, is used to set a line around the outside of an element, typically for highlighting purposes. Outlines do not affect the layout of the document.

34.What is the purpose of the `autocomplete` attribute in an HTML `<form>` element?

Answer:The `autocomplete` attribute is used to control whether a browser should automatically complete values in a form. It can take values like "on" or "off," influencing whether the browser should remember and fill in form field values based on user input history.

35.Explain the role of the `picture` element in HTML5.

Answer:The `<picture>` element is used for responsive images. It allows developers to provide multiple sources for an image and specify different images based on factors such as screen size, resolution, or other media conditions, enhancing the adaptability of images on different devices.

36.What is the purpose of the HTML `<cite>` element?

Answer:The `<cite>` element is used to reference the title of a creative work, such as a book, movie, or publication, within the text. It is often used to provide proper citation and semantic meaning to the cited content.

37.Explain the purpose of the `formaction` attribute in an HTML `<button>` element.

Answer:The `formaction` attribute in a `<button>` element is used to override the `action` attribute of the surrounding `<form>` element for that specific button. It allows the button to submit the form to a different URL than the one specified in the form's `action` attribute.

38.What is the purpose of the HTML `<mark>` element?

Answer:The `<mark>` element is used to highlight text within the context of a document. It is often employed to indicate a portion of text that is relevant or matches a search query.

39.Explain the role of the `target` attribute in the `<a>` tag.

Answer:The `target` attribute in the `<a>` tag is used to specify where the linked document should be opened. Common values include "_blank" (open in a new window or tab) and "_self" (open in the same frame or tab).

40.What is the purpose of the HTML `<fieldset>` and `<legend>` elements?

Answer:The `<fieldset>` element is used to group related form elements within a form, and the `<legend>` element provides a caption or title for the `<fieldset>`. It helps organize and label form controls for better accessibility and user understanding.

41.Explain the purpose of the `role` attribute in HTML.

Answer: The `role` attribute is used to define the purpose or type of an element for accessibility. It helps assistive technologies understand the structure and purpose of the content. For example, `<div role="navigation">` explicitly indicates a navigation section.

42.What is the purpose of the HTML `<meter>` element?

Answer: The `<meter>` element is used to represent a scalar measurement within a known range. It is often used for gauges, progress bars, or other situations where a value needs to be visually represented within a specific range.

43.Explain the purpose of the `translate` attribute in the `<html>` tag.

Answer: The `translate` attribute in the `<html>` tag is used to specify whether the content of an HTML document should be translated. It can take values such as "yes" or "no" to indicate whether the text content is eligible for translation.

44.What is the purpose of the HTML `<time>` element's `datetime` attribute?

Answer: The `datetime` attribute in the `<time>` element is used to provide machine-readable information about the date and time. It helps browsers and search engines understand and parse the time information accurately.

45.Explain the purpose of the `controls` attribute in the `<audio>` and `<video>` elements.

Answer: The `controls` attribute is used in the `<audio>` and `<video>` elements to display default playback controls to the user. These controls include play, pause, volume, and progress bar, enhancing the user experience for multimedia content.

46.What is the purpose of the HTML `<ruby>` and `<rt>` elements?

Answer: The `<ruby>` element is used to provide annotations for complex characters, such as those in East Asian languages. The `<rt>` element is used to define the pronunciation or additional information about the content enclosed by `<ruby>`.

47.Explain the purpose of the HTML `<dialog>` element.

Answer: The `<dialog>` element is used to create a modal or popup dialog box. It can be opened and closed using JavaScript, providing a way to display additional information, forms, or other content without navigating away from the current page.

48.What is the purpose of the `defer` and `async` attributes in the `<script>` tag?

Answer: The `defer` attribute in the `<script>` tag delays script execution until the HTML document has been fully parsed. The `async` attribute, on the other hand, allows the script to be downloaded asynchronously, and it is executed as soon as it is available, without waiting for the HTML parsing to complete.

49.Explain the purpose of the HTML `<code>` element.

Answer: The `<code>` element is used to define a piece of computer code within the text. It is often used to display code snippets, programming instructions, or any text that should be rendered in a monospaced font for better readability.

50.What is the purpose of the HTML `<wbr>` element?

Answer: The `<wbr>` (Word Break Opportunity) element is used to suggest a potential line break within a word. It is used to improve the layout and readability of long words or URLs by allowing browsers to break them at specific points.

51.Explain the purpose of the `crossorigin` attribute in the `<script>` tag when loading external scripts.

Answer: The `crossorigin` attribute is used in the `<script>` tag when loading external scripts from a different domain. It controls how the browser handles cross-origin requests for the script. Common values include "anonymous" and "use-credentials."

52.What is the purpose of the HTML `<bdi>` element?

Answer: The `<bdi>` (Bi-Directional Isolation) element is used to isolate a span of text that might be formatted in a different direction from the surrounding text. It helps maintain the text's directionality within a bidirectional text context.

53.Explain the purpose of the `defer` attribute in the `<style>` tag.

Answer: The `defer` attribute in the `<style>` tag is used to defer the rendering of the stylesheet until the HTML document has been fully parsed. This is similar to the `defer` attribute in the `<script>` tag but applies to stylesheets.

54.What is the purpose of the HTML `<figcaption>` element?

Answer: The `<figcaption>` element is used to provide a caption or description for the content within a `<figure>` element. It is often used in conjunction with images or multimedia content to provide additional context.

55.Explain the purpose of the `preload` attribute in the `<link>` tag.

Answer: The `preload` attribute in the `<link>` tag is used to provide a hint to the browser that a resource (such as a stylesheet or script) should be preloaded, even before it is needed. This can improve page performance by ensuring that critical resources are available when required.

56.What is the purpose of the HTML `<samp>` element?

Answer: The `<samp>` element is used to represent sample output or example computer code output. It is often used to display results from a program or script to provide visual examples.

57.Explain the purpose of the `download` attribute in the `<a>` tag.

Answer: The `download` attribute in the `<a>` tag is used to prompt the user to download a linked resource instead of navigating to it. It is often used with links to files, allowing users to save the file locally.

58.What is the purpose of the HTML `<var>` element?

Answer: The `<var>` element is used to represent the name of a variable in a mathematical expression or programming context. It is often used to provide semantic meaning to variable names within text.

59.Explain the purpose of the HTML `<input>` element's `list` attribute.

Answer: The `list` attribute in the `<input>` element is used to associate an `<input>` element with a `<datalist>` element. This allows users to choose from a list of predefined options while still allowing free-form input.

60.What is the purpose of the HTML `<progress>` element's `value` attribute?

Answer: The `value` attribute in the `<progress>` element is used to set or retrieve the current value of the progress bar. It represents the completion percentage of a task or the amount of progress made.

61.Explain the purpose of the `role` attribute in the context of accessibility.

Answer:The `role` attribute is used to define the purpose or type of an element, providing additional information for accessibility. It helps screen readers and other assistive technologies understand the intended role of an element, especially when the standard HTML semantics might not fully convey the meaning.

62.What is the purpose of the HTML `<picture>` element's `<source>` element?

Answer:The `<source>` element within the `<picture>` element is used to provide multiple sources or versions of an image based on different conditions, such as screen size, resolution, or media type. It allows developers to serve the most appropriate image for different scenarios.

63.Explain the purpose of the `aria-*` attributes in HTML.

Answer:The `aria-*` attributes, such as `aria-label` and `aria-describedby`, are part of the Accessible Rich Internet Applications (ARIA) specification. They are used to enhance the accessibility of web content by providing additional information about the roles, states, and properties of elements to assistive technologies.

64.What is the purpose of the HTML `<template>` element?

Answer:The `<template>` element is used to hold client-side content that should not be rendered when the page loads. It provides a mechanism for holding HTML content that can be cloned and inserted into the document using JavaScript. This is particularly useful for dynamic content generation.

65.Explain the purpose of the HTML5 `<nav>` element.

Answer:The `<nav>` element is used to define a navigation section on a web page. It is typically used to create navigation menus or links that help users navigate to different sections or pages within a website.

66.What is the purpose of the HTML `<pre>` element?

Answer:The `<pre>` element is used to define preformatted text, where whitespace, line breaks, and indentation are preserved. It is often used to display code snippets or text where the formatting is essential.

67.Explain the purpose of the `spellcheck` attribute in the `<textarea>` and `<input>` elements.

Answer:The `spellcheck` attribute is used to enable or disable spell checking for text entered into a `<textarea>` or `<input>` element. Setting `spellcheck="true"` enables spell checking, while `spellcheck="false"` disables it.

68.What is the purpose of the HTML `<rp>` and `<rt>` elements?

Answer:The `<rp>` (Ruby Parenthesis) and `<rt>` (Ruby Text) elements are used in ruby annotations for East Asian typography. `<rp>` is used to provide fallback parentheses for browsers that do not support ruby annotations, while `<rt>` is used to define the pronunciation or explanation of the preceding text.

69.Explain the purpose of the HTML `<dfn>` element.

Answer:The `<dfn>` (Definition) element is used to represent the defining instance of a term within a document. It is often used to mark up the term being defined, providing semantic meaning.

70.What is the purpose of the HTML `<s>` and `<del>` elements?

Answer:Both `<s>` and `<del>` elements are used to represent text that is no longer accurate or relevant. They are often used to indicate deleted or strikethrough text. The `<del>` element has additional semantic meaning, indicating that the text has been deleted or removed from the document.

71.Explain the purpose of the `sandbox` attribute in the `<iframe>` element.

Answer: The `sandbox` attribute in the `<iframe>` element is used to enable a restricted security sandbox for the content within the iframe. It restricts certain behaviors, such as form submission and script execution, to enhance security when embedding content from potentially untrusted sources.

72.What is the purpose of the HTML `<meter>` element's `min` and `max` attributes?

Answer: The `min` and `max` attributes in the `<meter>` element define the minimum and maximum values of the range that the meter represents. The `value` attribute within the `<meter>` element specifies the current value within that range.

73.Explain the purpose of the HTML `<small>` element.

Answer: The `<small>` element is used to represent small print or text that is smaller and less important than the surrounding text. It is often used for disclaimers, legal notices, or other text that should be visually de-emphasized.

74.What is the purpose of the `content` attribute in the `<meta>` tag?

Answer: The `content` attribute in the `<meta>` tag is used to provide the value associated with the specific metadata name or pragma. For example, `<meta name="viewport" content="width=device-width, initial-scale=1.0">` sets the viewport properties for responsive design.

75.Explain the purpose of the HTML `<colgroup>` and `<col>` elements.

Answer: The `<colgroup>` and `<col>` elements are used to apply styles to columns in an HTML table. The `<colgroup>` element contains one or more `<col>` elements, and attributes like `span` and `width` can be applied to define the properties of each column.

76.What is the purpose of the HTML `<progress>` element's `max` attribute?

Answer: The `max` attribute in the `<progress>` element defines the maximum value in the range that the progress bar represents. It works in conjunction with the `value` attribute, indicating the progress made relative to the maximum value.

77.Explain the purpose of the `list` attribute in the `<input>` element.

Answer: The `list` attribute in the `<input>` element is used to associate the input field with a `<datalist>` element. It provides a predefined list of options for user selection, allowing users to choose from the list or enter custom values.

78.What is the purpose of the HTML `<bdo>` element?

Answer: The `<bdo>` (Bi-Directional Override) element is used to override the text direction of its parent element. It is often used in situations where the text directionality needs to be explicitly set, especially in the context of bidirectional text.

79.Explain the purpose of the `default` attribute in the `<track>` element.

Answer: The `default` attribute in the `<track>` element is used to specify that the track should be enabled by default when the media element loads. It is commonly used with subtitles or captions to indicate the default language or track.

80.What is the purpose of the HTML `<cite>` element when used within the `<blockquote>` element?

Answer: When the `<cite>` element is used within the `<blockquote>` element, it is used to provide the citation or source of the quoted content. It indicates the origin or authorship of the quoted text.

81.Explain the purpose of the HTML `<iframe>` attribute `allowfullscreen`.

Answer: The `allowfullscreen` attribute in the `<iframe>` element is used to grant permission for the embedded content within the iframe (such as videos or maps) to enter full-screen mode when the user clicks on the fullscreen button.

82.What is the purpose of the HTML `<datalist>` element?

Answer: The `<datalist>` element is used to provide a set of predefined options for an `<input>` element. It allows users to choose from a list of options while still allowing them to enter custom values. The `<input>` is associated with the `<datalist>` using the `list` attribute.

83.Explain the purpose of the `ping` attribute in the `<a>` tag.

Answer: The `ping` attribute in the `<a>` tag is used to specify a space-separated list of URLs to which, when the hyperlink is followed, a ping request is sent. This can be used for tracking or logging purposes, providing information about the link navigation.

84.What is the purpose of the HTML `<abbr>` element's `title` attribute?

Answer: The `title` attribute in the `<abbr>` element is used to provide an expansion or explanation of the abbreviation. When the user hovers over the abbreviated text, the content of the `title` attribute is displayed as a tooltip.

85.Explain the purpose of the HTML `<main>` element.

Answer: The `<main>` element is used to define the main content of a document. It represents the primary content of the document, excluding headers, footers, and sidebars. The use of `<main>` enhances accessibility and helps assistive technologies identify the primary content.

86.What is the purpose of the HTML `<bdi>` element?

Answer: The `<bdi>` (Bi-Directional Isolation) element is used to isolate a span of text that might be formatted in a different direction from the surrounding text. It helps maintain the text's directionality within a bidirectional text context.

87.Explain the purpose of the HTML `<script>` element's `nonce` attribute.

Answer: The `nonce` attribute in the `<script>` element is used to provide a cryptographic nonce (number used once) to ensure that only authorized scripts are executed. It is often used as a security measure to prevent cross-site scripting (XSS) attacks.

88.What is the purpose of the `ismap` attribute in the HTML `<img>` element?

Answer: The `ismap` attribute in the `<img>` element is used to indicate that the image is part of a server-side image map. It is used in conjunction with the `usemap` attribute to define a clickable area within the image that corresponds to a specific URL.

89.Explain the purpose of the HTML `<time>` element's `pubdate` attribute.

Answer: The `pubdate` attribute in the `<time>` element is used to indicate that the time element represents the publication date of an article or content. It provides semantic meaning to the date within the context of publication.

90.What is the purpose of the HTML `<cite>` element when used outside of `<blockquote>`?

Answer: When the `<cite>` element is used outside of `<blockquote>`, it is used to reference the title of a creative work (such as a book or movie) or the name of a person or entity. It represents the cited title or name within the text.

91.Explain the purpose of the HTML `<details>` and `<summary>` elements.

Answer: The `<details>` element is used to create a disclosure widget, which allows users to show or hide additional information. The content that can be toggled is placed inside the `<details>` element, and the `<summary>` element provides a visible label or heading for the disclosed content.

92.What is the purpose of the `reversed` attribute in the HTML `<ol>` element?

Answer: The `reversed` attribute in the `<ol>` (ordered list) element is used to reverse the numbering of the list items. Normally, an ordered list starts with 1 and increments, but with `reversed`, it starts with a higher number and decrements.

93.Explain the purpose of the `defer` attribute in the `<audio>` and `<video>` elements.

Answer: The `defer` attribute in the `<audio>` and `<video>` elements is used to delay the loading and playback of the media until the rest of the document has been parsed. This can help improve page loading performance, especially when there are multiple media elements.

94.What is the purpose of the `longdesc` attribute in the HTML `<img>` element?

Answer: The `longdesc` attribute in the `<img>` element is used to provide a URL pointing to a long description of the image. It is used to offer more detailed information or context about the image, especially for users with visual impairments.

95.Explain the purpose of the HTML `<bdi>` element.

Answer: The `<bdi>` (Bi-Directional Isolation) element is used to isolate a span of text that might be formatted in a different direction from the surrounding text. It helps maintain the text's directionality within a bidirectional text context.

96.What is the purpose of the HTML `<noscript>` element?

Answer: The `<noscript>` element is used to provide alternate content that should be displayed if the user's browser does not support JavaScript or if JavaScript is disabled. It is commonly used to display a message asking users to enable JavaScript.

97.Explain the purpose of the HTML `<fieldset>` and `<legend>` elements.

Answer: The `<fieldset>` element is used to group related form elements within a form, and the `<legend>` element provides a caption or title for the `<fieldset>`. It helps organize and label form controls for better accessibility and user understanding.

98.What is the purpose of the `role` attribute in HTML, and how is it used?

Answer: The `role` attribute is used to define the purpose or type of an element for accessibility. It helps assistive technologies understand the structure and purpose of the content. For example, `<div role="navigation">` explicitly indicates a navigation section.

99.Explain the purpose of the HTML `<samp>` element.

Answer: The `<samp>` element is used to represent sample output or example computer code output. It is often used to display results from a program or script to provide visual examples.

100.What is the purpose of the HTML `<picture>` element?

Answer: The `<picture>` element is used for responsive images. It allows developers to provide multiple sources for an image and specify different images based on factors such as screen size, resolution, or other media conditions, enhancing the adaptability of images on different devices.

101.Explain the purpose of the `scrolling` attribute in the `<iframe>` element.

Answer: The `scrolling` attribute in the `<iframe>` element is used to control whether the iframe should display scrollbars. It can take values such as "yes," "no," or "auto" to determine the visibility of scrollbars within the iframe.

102.What is the purpose of the HTML `<output>` element?

Answer: The `<output>` element is used to represent the result of a calculation or user action on a form. It allows developers to display the output of a script or calculation and can be associated with form controls using the `for` attribute.

103.Explain the purpose of the `wrap` attribute in the `<textarea>` element.

Answer: The `wrap` attribute in the `<textarea>` element is used to control how the text within the textarea should wrap. It can take values like "soft" (text wraps at whitespace) or "hard" (text wraps at the specified column width), influencing the text layout.

104.What is the purpose of the `controlsList` attribute in the HTML `<audio>` and `<video>` elements?

Answer: The `controlsList` attribute in the `<audio>` and `<video>` elements is used to customize the set of controls that are displayed to the user. It allows developers to selectively show or hide specific media controls, enhancing the user interface.

105.Explain the purpose of the `translate` attribute in the HTML `<q>` element.

Answer: The `translate` attribute in the `<q>` element is used to control whether the content of the element should be translated. It can take values like "yes" or "no" to indicate whether the text content is eligible for translation.

106.What is the purpose of the HTML `<link>` element's `crossorigin` attribute?

Answer: The `crossorigin` attribute in the `<link>` element is used to specify how the browser should handle cross-origin requests for linked resources, such as stylesheets or fonts. It can take values like "anonymous" or "use-credentials."

107.Explain the purpose of the HTML `<figcaption>` element.

Answer: The `<figcaption>` element is used to provide a caption or description for the content within a `<figure>` element. It is often used in conjunction with images or multimedia content to provide additional context.

108.What is the purpose of the HTML `<wbr>` element?

Answer: The `<wbr>` (Word Break Opportunity) element is used to suggest a potential line break within a word. It is used to improve the layout and readability of long words or URLs by allowing browsers to break them at specific points.

109.Explain the purpose of the HTML `<section>` element.

Answer: The `<section>` element is used to define a section within an HTML document. It is often used to group related content together and provide semantic meaning to the structure of the document.

110.What is the purpose of the `itemprop` attribute in HTML?

Answer: The `itemprop` attribute is used in the context of microdata and the Schema.org vocabulary. It is applied to HTML elements to provide additional information about the specific property of an item. It helps search engines and other applications better understand the content's meaning.

111.Explain the purpose of the HTML `<cite>` element when used within the `<figure>` element.

Answer:When the `<cite>` element is used within the `<figure>` element, it is typically used to reference the source or author of the content within the figure. It provides attribution for the content presented within the `<figure>`.

112.What is the purpose of the `download` attribute in the HTML `<a>` tag?

Answer:The `download` attribute in the `<a>` tag is used to prompt the user to download a linked resource instead of navigating to it. It is often used with links to files, allowing users to save the file locally.

113.Explain the purpose of the `autofocus` attribute in the HTML `<input>` element.

Answer:The `autofocus` attribute in the `<input>` element is used to automatically focus on the input field when the page loads. This can improve the user experience by placing the cursor in the input field, ready for user input.

114.What is the purpose of the HTML `<meter>` element's `low`, `high`, and `optimum` attributes?

Answer:The `low`, `high`, and `optimum` attributes in the `<meter>` element define the ranges for a gauge or progress bar. The `low` attribute specifies the lower bound, `high` specifies the upper bound, and `optimum` specifies the optimal value within the range.

115.Explain the purpose of the HTML `<template>` element.

Answer:The `<template>` element is used to hold client-side content that should not be rendered when the page loads. It provides a mechanism for holding HTML content that can be cloned and inserted into the document using JavaScript. This is particularly useful for dynamic content generation.

116.What is the purpose of the HTML `<mark>` element?

Answer:The `<mark>` element is used to highlight text within the context of a document. It is often employed to indicate a portion of text that is relevant or matches a search query.

117.Explain the purpose of the HTML `<kbd>` element.

Answer:The `<kbd>` element is used to represent keyboard input. It is often used to enclose text that represents user input from a keyboard, such as key names or keyboard shortcuts.

118.What is the purpose of the `defer` attribute in the HTML `<iframe>` element?

Answer:The `defer` attribute in the `<iframe>` element is used to delay the loading of the iframe's content until the rest of the document has been fully parsed. It helps improve the overall page loading performance.

119.Explain the purpose of the `open` attribute in the HTML `<details>` element.

Answer:The `open` attribute in the `<details>` element is used to specify that the additional information within the details element should be visible or open by default when the page loads.

120.What is the purpose of the HTML `<b>` and `<strong>` elements?

Answer:Both `<b>` and `<strong>` elements are used to apply bold formatting to text. However, `<strong>` carries additional semantic meaning, indicating that the enclosed text is of strong importance or importance for emphasis.

121.Explain the purpose of the HTML `<hgroup>` element.

Answer: The `<hgroup>` element is used to group together a set of heading elements (`<h1>` through `<h6>`) when they are part of a multi-level heading structure. It helps provide a hierarchical structure to the headings within a section of content.

122.What is the purpose of the HTML `<meter>` element's `low` attribute?

Answer: The `low` attribute in the `<meter>` element specifies the lower bound of the range for a gauge or progress bar. It indicates the minimum value within the range that the meter represents.

123.Explain the purpose of the `autoplay` attribute in the HTML `<audio>` and `<video>` elements.

Answer: The `autoplay` attribute in the `<audio>` and `<video>` elements is used to automatically start playback of the media content when the page loads. It allows developers to provide a seamless multimedia experience without requiring user interaction.

124.What is the purpose of the HTML `<cite>` element when used within the `<time>` element?

Answer: When the `<cite>` element is used within the `<time>` element, it is used to reference the source or authorship of the time element. It provides attribution for the time-related content within the document.

125.Explain the purpose of the HTML `<kbd>` and `<samp>` elements.

Answer: The `<kbd>` element is used to represent keyboard input, while the `<samp>` element is used to represent sample output or example computer code output. They are often used together to illustrate user input and the resulting output in a code-related context.

126.What is the purpose of the `enctype` attribute in the HTML `<form>` element?

Answer: The `enctype` attribute in the `<form>` element is used to specify the encoding type used when the form data is submitted to the server. Common values include "application/x-www-form-urlencoded" and "multipart/form-data" for handling different types of form data.

127.Explain the purpose of the HTML `<s>` element.

Answer: The `<s>` element is used to represent text that is no longer accurate or relevant, indicating that the content within it has been "struck through" or marked for deletion. It is often used for indicating deleted text.

128.What is the purpose of the HTML `<canvas>` element?

Answer: The `<canvas>` element is used to create graphics, drawings, and animations on a web page using JavaScript. It provides an area where developers can use a scripting language (usually JavaScript) to draw shapes, images, and manipulate pixels.

129.Explain the purpose of the `sandbox` attribute in the HTML `<iframe>` element.

Answer: The `sandbox` attribute in the `<iframe>` element is used to create a sandbox environment for the content within the iframe. It restricts certain behaviors, such as form submission and script execution, to enhance security when embedding content from potentially untrusted sources.

130.What is the purpose of the HTML `<datalist>` element's `<option>` elements?

Answer: The `<datalist>` element's `<option>` elements are used to define the list of predefined options that can be associated with an `<input>` element. Users can choose from these options, and the selected value is then submitted with the form.

131.Explain the purpose of the HTML `<article>` element.

Answer: The `<article>` element is used to represent a self-contained piece of content within a document. It can be an article, blog post, forum post, or any other content that can be distributed and reused independently.

132.What is the purpose of the HTML `<command>` element?

Answer: The `<command>` element was part of an obsolete HTML specification and was used to define a command that users could invoke through the browser's user interface. It has been deprecated in favor of more modern approaches, and its usage is not recommended.

133.Explain the purpose of the `defer` attribute in the HTML `<details>` element.

Answer: The `defer` attribute in the `<details>` element is used to delay the loading and rendering of the content within the details element until the user activates it (typically by clicking). This can help improve page loading performance by loading content only when needed.

134.What is the purpose of the HTML `<rp>` element?

Answer: The `<rp>` (Ruby Parenthesis) element is used in ruby annotations for East Asian typography. It provides parentheses that are displayed in browsers that do not support ruby annotations. It is typically used in conjunction with the `<ruby>` element.

135.Explain the purpose of the `sizes` attribute in the HTML `<link>` tag for responsive web design.

Answer: The `sizes` attribute in the `<link>` tag is used in conjunction with the `srcset` attribute to specify the sizes of the images referenced by the `srcset` attribute. It helps browsers determine the most appropriate image to download based on the device's screen size and resolution in responsive web design.

136.What is the purpose of the HTML `<ins>` element?

Answer: The `<ins>` element is used to represent inserted text or content within a document. It typically renders as underlined text, indicating that the content has been added or inserted.

137.Explain the purpose of the `accept-charset` attribute in the HTML `<form>` element.

Answer: The `accept-charset` attribute in the `<form>` element is used to specify the character encodings that the server can accept when processing the form submission. It helps ensure proper character encoding for form data.

138.What is the purpose of the HTML `<abbr>` element's `title` attribute?

Answer: The `title` attribute in the `<abbr>` element is used to provide an expansion or explanation of the abbreviation. When users hover over the abbreviated text, the content of the `title` attribute is displayed as a tooltip.

139.Explain the purpose of the HTML `<aside>` element.

Answer: The `<aside>` element is used to define content that is tangentially related to the content around it. It is often used for sidebars, pull quotes, or other content that is considered supplementary to the main content.

140.What is the purpose of the HTML `<summary>` element within the `<details>` element?

Answer: The `<summary>` element within the `<details>` element is used to provide a visible label or heading for the content within the details element. It serves as a user-friendly way to reveal or hide additional information.

141.Explain the purpose of the HTML `<map>` element.

Answer: The `<map>` element is used in conjunction with the `<area>` element to create image maps. Image maps allow specific regions of an image to be clickable, each associated with a different hyperlink or action.

142.What is the purpose of the `async` and `defer` attributes in the HTML `<script>` element?

Answer: The `async` attribute in the `<script>` element is used to indicate that the script should be executed asynchronously, allowing it to run while the HTML parsing continues. The `defer` attribute, on the other hand, defers script execution until after the HTML parsing is complete, maintaining order if multiple scripts are present.

143.Explain the purpose of the HTML `<output>` element's `for` attribute.

Answer: The `for` attribute in the `<output>` element is used to associate the output element with a specific form element. It specifies the ID of the related form control, indicating that the output represents the result or output of that form control.

144.What is the purpose of the `loading` attribute in the HTML `<img>` element?

Answer: The `loading` attribute in the `<img>` element is used to control the loading behavior of the image. It can take values like "lazy" to defer loading until it's about to come into the viewport, improving page performance.

145.Explain the purpose of the HTML `<hgroup>` element.

Answer: The `<hgroup>` element is used to group together multiple heading elements (`<h1>` through `<h6>`) when they are part of a heading structure. It helps provide a hierarchical structure to the headings within a section of content.

146.What is the purpose of the HTML `<samp>` element?

Answer: The `<samp>` element is used to represent sample output or example computer code output. It is often used to display results from a program or script to provide visual examples.

147.Explain the purpose of the `contenteditable` attribute in HTML.

Answer: The `contenteditable` attribute is used to make the content of an element editable by the user. When set to "true," the user can edit the content directly within the element, turning it into an interactive editing area.

148.What is the purpose of the HTML `<fieldset>` and `<legend>` elements?

Answer: The `<fieldset>` element is used to group related form elements within a form, and the `<legend>` element provides a caption or title for the `<fieldset>`. It helps organize and label form controls for better accessibility and user understanding.

149.Explain the purpose of the `sizes` attribute in the HTML `<img>` element.

Answer: The `sizes` attribute in the `<img>` element is used to specify the size of the image as a media condition in a responsive design. It helps browsers determine the most appropriate image to download based on the device's screen size and resolution.

150.What is the purpose of the HTML `<cite>` element when used within the `<figure>` element?

Answer: When the `<cite>` element is used within the `<figure>` element, it is typically used to reference the source or author of the content within the figure. It provides attribution for the content presented within the `<figure>`.

CSS

1.What is CSS, and what is its role in web development?

Answer:

CSS stands for Cascading Style Sheets. It is a style sheet language used for describing the look and formatting of a document written in HTML or XML. CSS allows developers to control the layout, colors, fonts, and other visual aspects of a web page, enabling a separation between content and presentation.

2.Explain the concept of "Cascading" in CSS.

Answer:

The term "Cascading" in CSS refers to the order of priority or precedence when multiple styles are applied to an HTML element. Styles can be defined in various ways, such as inline styles, internal styles (within the `<style>` tag in the HTML document), and external styles (in a separate CSS file). The cascade determines the order of importance, with inline styles having the highest priority, followed by internal styles and then external styles.

3.What is the box model in CSS?

Answer:

The box model in CSS describes the structure of an HTML element as a rectangular box. It consists of content, padding, border, and margin. The content is the actual text or media within the element, padding is the space between the content and the border, the border surrounds the padding, and the margin is the space outside the border.

4.Differentiate between `margin` and `padding` in CSS.

Answer:

-Margin: It is the space outside the border of an element. It creates space between the element and its surrounding elements.

-Padding: It is the space between the content of an element and its border. It provides internal spacing within the element.

5.Explain the difference between `display: none;` and `visibility: hidden;`.

Answer:

-`display: none;`: This property hides the element completely, and the space it occupies is removed from the document flow. It's as if the element doesn't exist.

-`visibility: hidden;`: This property hides the element, but it still occupies space in the document flow. The element is visually hidden, but its space is preserved.

6.What is the significance of the z-index property in CSS?

Answer:

The `z-index` property in CSS is used to control the stacking order of positioned elements. Elements with a higher `z-index` value are displayed in front of elements with a lower `z-index`. This property is particularly useful when dealing with overlapping elements or layers.

7.What is the CSS box-sizing property, and how does it affect layout?

Answer:

The `box-sizing` property in CSS determines how the total width and height of an element are calculated. The two main values are:

  -`content-box` (default): The width and height include only the content, not padding, border, or margin.

  -`border-box`: The width and height include content, padding, and border, but not the margin. This can simplify layout calculations.

8.Explain the difference between `position: relative`, `position: absolute`, and `position: fixed`.

Answer:

-`position: relative`: Positions an element relative to its normal position in the document flow. It can be moved using properties like `top`, `right`, `bottom`, and `left`.

-`position: absolute`: Positions an element relative to its nearest positioned (not static) ancestor. If there is no such ancestor, it's positioned relative to the initial containing block.

-`position: fixed`: Positions an element relative to the browser window. It remains fixed even when the page is scrolled.

9.What is the purpose of the `float` property in CSS, and how does it work?

Answer:

The `float` property in CSS is used for positioning and alignment of elements. When an element is floated, it is taken out of the normal flow of the document and moved to the left or right until it reaches the edge of its containing element or another floated element. This is commonly used for creating layouts where elements can be positioned side by side.

10.Explain the concept of responsive web design and how media queries are used.

Answer:

Responsive web design is an approach that ensures web pages render well on a variety of devices and window or screen sizes. Media queries in CSS are used to apply different styles based on the characteristics of the device, such as its width, height, and resolution. This allows developers to create designs that adapt to various devices, providing a seamless user experience across desktops, tablets, and mobile phones.

11.What is the CSS specificity and how is it calculated?

Answer:

CSS specificity is a mechanism that determines which styles will be applied to an element when multiple conflicting styles exist. Specificity is calculated based on the following factors:

- Inline styles have the highest specificity.

- IDs contribute more specificity than classes or attributes.

- Elements and pseudo-elements have the lowest specificity.

The specificity is represented as a four-part value, like "a, b, c, d," where each part corresponds to the importance of a different selector type.

12.Explain the purpose of the CSS `transform` property and give an example of its usage.

Answer:

The `transform` property in CSS is used to apply transformations to elements. This can include rotating, scaling, translating (moving), and skewing elements. For example, to rotate an element by 45 degrees, you can use:

```
transform: rotate(45deg);
```

13.What is the CSS `box-shadow` property, and how is it used to create shadows around elements?

Answer:

The `box-shadow` property is used to add a shadow effect to an element's box. It takes values for the horizontal and vertical offset, blur radius, spread distance, and the color of the shadow. For example:

```
box-shadow: 5px 5px 10px #888888;
```

14.Explain the difference between the `:nth-child` and `:nth-of-type` pseudo-classes.

Answer:

-`:nth-child`: Selects elements based on their position among a group of siblings, regardless of their element type.

-`:nth-of-type`: Selects elements based on their position among a group of siblings of the same element type.

For instance, `:nth-child(2)` would select the second child of its parent, regardless of its element type, while `:nth-of-type(2)` would select the second child only if it's the same type as the specified selector.

15.What is the CSS `rem` unit, and how does it differ from `em`?

Answer:

The `rem` unit stands for "root em" and is relative to the font size of the root element (usually the `<html>` element). In contrast, the `em` unit is relative to the font size of the parent element. Using `rem` provides a more consistent and predictable way to size elements, especially in the context of responsive web design.

16.How does the CSS `clip-path` property work, and what can it be used for?

Answer:

The `clip-path` property in CSS is used to create complex shapes by clipping an element. It defines the visible portion of an element and hides the rest. It can be used for various effects, including creating non-rectangular shapes, image masking, and more.

17.What is the purpose of the CSS `filter` property, and how can it be applied to an element?

Answer:

The `filter` property in CSS is used to apply graphical effects like blur, brightness, contrast, grayscale, etc., to elements. For example, to apply a 50% blur effect, you can use:

```
filter: blur(5px);
```

18.Explain the concept of the CSS `currentColor` keyword.

Answer:

   The `currentColor` keyword in CSS is used to set the value of a property to the computed value of the `color` property of the element. It allows for dynamic adaptation of properties like border or background color to the text color of the element.

19.What is the purpose of the CSS `counter` and `content` properties?

Answer:

   The `counter` and `content` properties are used in conjunction with the CSS Counter feature. The `counter` property increments a counter, and the `content` property is used to insert generated content, including the value of a counter, into an element. This is often used in conjunction with the `::before` and `::after` pseudo-elements.

20.How does the CSS `object-fit` property work, and when might it be useful?

Answer:

   The `object-fit` property in CSS is used to specify how an `<img>` or `<video>` should be resized within its container. It can take values like `contain` (maintains aspect ratio, fits within the container), and `cover` (maintains aspect ratio, covers the entire container). This property is particularly useful for responsive design when dealing with media elements.

21.What is the purpose of the CSS `user-select` property, and how does it affect text selection?

Answer:

The `user-select` property in CSS controls the user's ability to select text. It can take values like `auto`, `none`, `text`, and `all`. For example, setting `user-select: none;` prevents text selection, while `user-select: all;` allows the user to select all text within an element.

22.Explain the CSS `transition` property and how it is used to create smooth animations.

Answer:

The `transition` property in CSS is used to smoothly transition the changes in style properties over a specified duration. It is commonly used for creating animations when an element undergoes a state change. For instance:

```
transition: width 0.5s ease-in-out;
```

23.What is the purpose of the CSS `line-height` property, and how does it affect text layout?

Answer:

The `line-height` property in CSS defines the space between lines within a block-level element containing text. It can be set as a numeric value, a percentage, or a specific length. A higher `line-height` value increases the space between lines, improving readability.

24.Explain the concept of CSS sprites and how they can be beneficial for web performance.

Answer:

CSS sprites involve combining multiple images into a single image and using CSS to display only the portion needed for a particular element. This reduces the number of server requests, improving page load times. The background position is then adjusted to display the appropriate image for a given element.

25.What is the purpose of the CSS `unicode-bidi` property, and when might it be used?

Answer:

The `unicode-bidi` property in CSS is used to control the directionality of text within an element. It is often used in conjunction with the `direction` property. For example, setting `unicode-bidi: embed;` allows an element to override the bidirectional algorithm and display text in a specific direction.

26.Explain the difference between `visibility: hidden;` and `opacity: 0;`.

Answer:

-`visibility: hidden;`: The element is hidden, but it still occupies space in the layout.

-`opacity: 0;`: The element is transparent, and it does not occupy space. However, it still interacts with the page, and its events are still triggered.

27.What is the purpose of the CSS `box-decoration-break` property?

Answer:

The `box-decoration-break` property in CSS is used to control the breaking behavior of boxes when split across multiple lines. It can take values like `slice` (default) and `clone`. Setting it to `clone` ensures that the box is fully rendered on each line, while `slice` allows the box to be split, with the style applied separately to each fragment.

28.How does the CSS `will-change` property work, and when might it be beneficial for performance?

Answer:

The `will-change` property in CSS is used to inform the browser about the types of changes an element is expected to undergo. This allows the browser to optimize the rendering process. It can be beneficial for performance when certain styles, like transformations or opacity, are known to change dynamically.

29.What is the purpose of the CSS `:not()` pseudo-class, and how is it used in selectors?

Answer:

The `:not()` pseudo-class in CSS is used to select elements that do not match a specified selector. For example, `:not(.special)` would select all elements that do not have the class "special."

30.Explain the concept of the CSS `calc()` function and provide an example of its usage.

Answer:

The `calc()` function in CSS is used to perform calculations within style property values. It is particularly useful for dynamic sizing. For example:

```css
width: calc(50% - 20px);
```

This sets the width to 50% of the container minus 20 pixels.

31.What is the purpose of the CSS `mask` property, and how can it be used for image masking?

Answer:

The `mask` property in CSS is used for image masking. It allows you to apply a mask to an element, revealing only the portion of the element that is covered by the mask. The mask itself can be an image or a gradient.

```css
mask: url('mask-image.png') no-repeat center / contain;
```

32.Explain the concept of CSS grid layout and its advantages over traditional layout methods.

Answer:

CSS Grid Layout is a two-dimensional layout system for the web. It allows for the creation of complex layouts with rows and columns, providing better control over both the placement and alignment of elements. Unlike traditional layout methods like floats or positioning, CSS Grid simplifies the design of responsive and intricate page layouts.

33.What is the CSS `currentColor` keyword, and how is it used?

Answer:

The `currentColor` keyword in CSS is used to represent the computed value of the `color` property. It is often used in conjunction with other properties, like `border` or `box-shadow`, to dynamically match the element's text color.

```
border: 2px solid currentColor;
```

34.Explain the purpose of the CSS `pointer-events` property.

Answer:

The `pointer-events` property in CSS is used to control under what circumstances an element can be the target of mouse events. It can take values like `auto`, `none`, `visible`, and `visiblePainted`. For example, setting `pointer-events: none;` makes an element non-interactive, allowing events to pass through to the elements beneath it.

35.How does the CSS `contain` property work, and what are its potential benefits for performance optimization?

Answer:

The `contain` property in CSS is used to indicate that an element's subtree is independent of the rest of the page. It can take values like `layout`, `style`, `paint`, and `size`. This can help the browser optimize rendering by isolating certain elements from the global styles and layout, potentially improving performance.

36.Explain the concept of CSS custom properties (variables) and their advantages.

Answer:

CSS custom properties, also known as variables, allow developers to define reusable values in CSS. They are declared using the `--` prefix and can be used within the stylesheet. Custom properties bring modularity and ease of maintenance to stylesheets, enabling changes to be made in a central location.

```css
:root {
  --primary-color: #3498db;
}

.element {
  color: var(--primary-color);
}
```

37.What is the CSS `attr()` function, and how can it be used?

Answer:

The `attr()` function in CSS is used to retrieve the value of an HTML attribute and use it as a property value. It is often used in conjunction with the `content` property in pseudo-elements to insert content based on an attribute value.

```css
span::before {
  content: attr(data-text);
}
```

38.Explain the purpose of the CSS `mix-blend-mode` property and provide an example of its usage.

Answer:

The `mix-blend-mode` property in CSS is used to specify how an element's content should blend with its background. It takes values like `normal`, `multiply`, `screen`, etc. For example:

```css
.element {
  mix-blend-mode: multiply;
}
```

39.What is the purpose of the CSS `:focus` pseudo-class, and how can it be used for styling interactive elements?

Answer:

The `:focus` pseudo-class in CSS is used to select and style an element that is currently in focus. It is commonly used to provide visual feedback for interactive elements like form inputs when they receive keyboard focus.

```css
input:focus {
  border: 2px solid #ff0000;
}
```

40.Explain the concept of CSS feature queries using `@supports`.

Answer:

CSS feature queries using `@supports` allow developers to conditionally apply styles based on whether a browser supports a particular CSS feature. This helps in creating fallbacks or applying styles selectively. For example:

```css
@supports (display: grid) {
  .container {
    display: grid;
  }
}
```

41.What is the purpose of the CSS `shape-outside` property, and how can it be used?

Answer:

The `shape-outside` property in CSS is used to control the flow of content around a non-rectangular shape. It is often used in conjunction with floated elements or images to create text wrapping around custom shapes, such as circles or polygons.

```css
img {

  shape-outside: circle(50%);

}
```

42.Explain the concept of the CSS `backface-visibility` property.

Answer:

The `backface-visibility` property in CSS is used to determine whether the back face of an element should be visible when it is rotated in 3D space. It can take values like `visible` or `hidden`. This property is commonly used in 3D transformations to control whether the back face of an element is visible during animations.

```css
.box {

  transform: rotateY(180deg);

  backface-visibility: hidden;
```

```
}
```
```

43.What is the purpose of the CSS `grid-template-areas` property, and how is it used in CSS Grid Layout?


Answer:

The `grid-template-areas` property in CSS Grid Layout is used to define named grid areas within the layout. It allows for the creation of complex layouts with visual representation in the code. Each area name corresponds to a grid item, and the layout is defined using these area names.


```css
.container {
  display: grid;
  grid-template-areas:
    "header header header"
    "sidebar main main"
    "footer footer footer";
}
```

44.Explain the concept of the CSS `will-change` property and how it can be used for performance optimization.

Answer:
```

The `will-change` property in CSS is used to inform the browser that an element is expected to change in a specific way, allowing the browser to optimize the rendering process. It is often used with properties like `transform` or `opacity` that are known to trigger costly repaints or reflows.

```css
.element {
  will-change: transform;
}
```

45.What is the purpose of the CSS `:empty` pseudo-class, and how can it be used in selectors?

Answer:

The `:empty` pseudo-class in CSS is used to select elements that have no children, including text nodes or other elements. It is often used in conjunction with other selectors to style or manipulate elements based on their content.

```css
p:empty {
  display: none;
}
```

46.Explain the concept of the CSS `contain: paint` property and its impact on rendering performance.

Answer:

The `contain: paint` property in CSS is used to indicate that an element's subtree is independent of layout and style changes. It informs the browser that the element's painted output does not depend on layout or style changes, potentially allowing the browser to optimize rendering performance.

```css
.element {

  contain: paint;

}
```

47.What is the purpose of the CSS `inset` shorthand property, and how is it used for positioning?

Answer:

The `inset` shorthand property in CSS is used to set all four positioning properties (`top`, `right`, `bottom`, and `left`) in a single declaration. It simplifies the syntax for positioning elements.

```css
.box {
  inset: 10px 20px 30px 40px;
}
```

48.Explain the concept of CSS flex containers and flex items.

Answer:

Flexbox is a layout model in CSS that is used to design a one-dimensional layout along a single axis (either horizontally or vertically). The container becomes a flex container, and the child elements become flex items. Flex properties are applied to the container and items to control the layout, alignment, and distribution of space.

```css
.container {
  display: flex;
  justify-content: space-between;
}
```

49. What is the CSS `resize` property used for, and how does it work?

Answer:

The `resize` property in CSS is used to control whether an element is resizable by the user. It is commonly used with `<textarea>` and `<input>` elements. The property can take values like `none`, `both`, `horizontal`, and `vertical`.

```css
textarea {
  resize: both;
}
```

50. Explain the purpose of the CSS `mask-image` property and how it is used for image masking.

Answer:

The `mask-image` property in CSS is used to specify an image or gradient as a mask for an element. It works in conjunction with other mask-related properties to create complex masking effects.

```css
.element {
  mask-image: url('mask-image.png');
}
```

51.What is the purpose of the CSS `gap` property in Grid Layout, and how does it differ from `grid-gap`?

Answer:

The `gap` property in CSS Grid Layout is used to set the gap between grid items both row-wise and column-wise. It is a shorthand property that combines `row-gap` and `column-gap`. In contrast, the `grid-gap` property is the older syntax for achieving the same result.

```css
.container {
  gap: 10px;
}
```

52.Explain the concept of CSS variables inheritance and how it impacts styling.

Answer:

CSS variables, also known as custom properties, can be inherited. If a variable is defined in a parent element, its value will be inherited by its children. This allows for a cascading effect where variables can be defined globally and inherited throughout the document, simplifying maintenance.

```css
:root {
  --primary-color: #3498db;
}


.child {
  color: var(--primary-color);
}
```

53. What is the purpose of the CSS `grid-auto-flow` property in Grid Layout?

Answer:

The `grid-auto-flow` property in CSS Grid Layout is used to control the placement of grid items when they are not explicitly placed in the grid. It can take values like `row`, `column`, `row dense`, and `column dense`. The `dense` value helps in filling in any empty cells in the grid.

```css
.container {
  grid-auto-flow: column dense;
}
```

54. Explain the concept of the CSS `object-position` property and its use with images.

Answer:

The `object-position` property in CSS is used to set the alignment of the content inside the container element. It is often used with images to control their positioning within a containing element.

```
img {
  object-position: center top;
}
```

55.What is the purpose of the CSS `currentColor` keyword, and how is it used?

Answer:

The `currentColor` keyword in CSS represents the computed value of the `color` property. It is often used in conjunction with other properties, like `border` or `box-shadow`, to dynamically match the element's text color.

```
.element {
  border: 2px solid currentColor;
}
```

56.Explain the CSS `aspect-ratio` property and how it can be used.

Answer:

The `aspect-ratio` property in CSS is used to set the aspect ratio of an element. It is particularly useful for maintaining a specific aspect ratio, such as 16:9 for videos. The property can take values like `auto`, a ratio (e.g., `16/9`), or a keyword (e.g., `auto 1/1`).

```
.video-container {
  aspect-ratio: 16/9;
}
```

57.What is the purpose of the CSS `min-content` and `max-content` values in sizing properties?

Answer:

In CSS sizing properties like `width` or `height`, `min-content` represents the minimum size an element can be while still fitting its content, and `max-content` represents the maximum size an element can be without overflowing. These values are useful for creating flexible and responsive layouts.

```css
.element {
  width: min-content;
}
```

58.Explain the CSS `unicode-range` property and its use with web fonts.

Answer:

The `unicode-range` property in CSS is used to specify the range of Unicode characters supported by a font face. It is often used with web fonts to define subsets of characters to download, reducing the overall font file size and improving performance.

```css
@font-face {
  font-family: 'CustomFont';
  src: url('custom-font.woff') format('woff');
  unicode-range: U+0000-00FF;
}
```

59.What is the purpose of the CSS `white-space` property, and how does it affect text layout?

Answer:

The `white-space` property in CSS is used to control how white spaces inside an element are handled. It can take values like `normal`, `nowrap`, `pre`, and `pre-line`. For example, setting `white-space: nowrap;` prevents text from wrapping to the next line.

```css
p {
  white-space: nowrap;
}
```

60.Explain the concept of CSS pseudo-elements and provide examples of their usage.

Answer:

CSS pseudo-elements are used to style certain parts of an element. They are denoted by the double colons (`::`) syntax. Examples include `::before` and `::after`. They are often used to insert content, create decorative elements, or style specific parts of an element.

```css
p::before {
  content: '\2022'; /* Bullet point */
  margin-right: 8px;
}
```

61. What is the CSS `object-fit` property, and how does it affect the sizing of replaced elements like images or videos?

Answer:

The `object-fit` property in CSS is used to specify how a replaced element, such as an image or video, should be resized to fit its container. It can take values like `fill`, `contain`, `cover`, etc. For example, setting `object-fit: cover;` will make the replaced element cover the entire container while maintaining its aspect ratio.

```css
img {
  object-fit: cover;
}
```

62. Explain the purpose of the CSS `currentColor` keyword, and provide an example of its usage.

Answer:

The `currentColor` keyword in CSS represents the computed value of the `color` property. It can be used in various properties to dynamically inherit and apply the text color of an element.


```css
.box {
  border: 2px solid currentColor;
}
```

63. What is the CSS `:root` pseudo-class, and how is it used in the context of CSS variables?

Answer:

The `:root` pseudo-class in CSS selects the highest-level parent element, typically the `<html>` element. It is commonly used to define global CSS variables that can be accessed throughout the document.

```css
:root {
  --primary-color: #3498db;
}


.element {
  color: var(--primary-color);
}
```

64. Explain the concept of the CSS `drop-shadow` property and how it can be used for creating box shadows.

Answer:

The `drop-shadow` property in CSS is used to apply a drop shadow to an element, similar to the `box-shadow` property. However, it is specifically designed for creating shadows around an alpha-masked image or object.

```css
.element {
  filter: drop-shadow(5px 5px 10px #888888);
}
```

65. What is the purpose of the CSS `outline` property, and how does it differ from `border`?

Answer:

The `outline` property in CSS is used to create a visible border around an element without affecting its layout. It is often used for focus states and accessibility. Unlike `border`, the `outline` does not take up space, and it does not have individual properties for width, style, and color.

```css
.element {
  outline: 2px solid red;
}
```

66. Explain the CSS `word-wrap` property and its role in handling long words or strings.

Answer:

The `word-wrap` property in CSS is used to control whether long words or strings should be broken and wrapped onto the next line. It can take values like `normal` (default) and `break-word`. Setting `word-wrap: break-word;` allows long words to break and wrap to the next line within the container.

```css
p {
  word-wrap: break-word;
}
```

67. What is the purpose of the CSS `mix-blend-mode` property, and how does it affect the blending of elements?

Answer:

The `mix-blend-mode` property in CSS is used to specify how the content of an element should blend with its background. It can take values like `normal`, `multiply`, `screen`, etc. This property is often used in creative designs to achieve various blending effects.

```css
.element {
  mix-blend-mode: overlay;
}
```

68. Explain the concept of the CSS `currentColor` keyword, and how is it used in conjunction with SVGs?

Answer:

The `currentColor` keyword in CSS is used to represent the computed value of the `color` property. In the context of SVGs, it can be used to dynamically apply the text color to parts of the SVG.

```css
svg {
  fill: currentColor;
  stroke: currentColor;
}
```

69. What is the purpose of the CSS `initial` keyword, and how is it used in property values?

Answer:

The `initial` keyword in CSS is used to set a property to its default or initial value. It can be useful when resetting a property to its standard value, especially within specific styles or in the context of CSS resets.

```css
.element {
  margin: initial;
}
```

70. Explain the CSS `contain` property and how it can be used for layout optimization.

Answer:

The `contain` property in CSS is used to indicate that an element's subtree is independent of layout, style, or paint changes. It can take values like `layout`, `style`, `paint`, and `size`. Using `contain` can help browsers optimize rendering performance by isolating specific elements from global styles or layout changes.

```css
.element {
  contain: layout;
}
```

71.What is the purpose of the CSS `aspect-ratio` property, and how can it be used in responsive design?

Answer:

The `aspect-ratio` property in CSS is used to set the aspect ratio of an element, which is the ratio of its width to its height. It is particularly useful in responsive design to maintain specific proportions. The property can take values like `auto`, a ratio (e.g., `16/9`), or a keyword (e.g., `auto 1/1`).

```css
.video-container {
  aspect-ratio: 16/9;
}
```

72.Explain the CSS `currentColor` keyword and provide an example of its usage with pseudo-elements.

Answer:

The `currentColor` keyword in CSS represents the computed value of the `color` property. It is often used in conjunction with pseudo-elements to dynamically inherit and apply the text color of an element.

```css
.element::before {
  content: '\2022'; /* Bullet point */
  color: currentColor;
  margin-right: 8px;
}
```

73.What is the purpose of the CSS `will-change` property, and how can it be used to improve animation performance?

Answer:

The `will-change` property in CSS is used to inform the browser that an element is expected to change in a specific way, allowing the browser to optimize the rendering process. It is often used with properties like `transform` or `opacity` that are known to trigger costly repaints or reflows, improving animation performance.

```css
.element {
  will-change: transform;
}
```

74.Explain the concept of the CSS `pointer-events` property and how it can be used in interactive design.

Answer:

The `pointer-events` property in CSS is used to control under what circumstances an element can be the target of mouse events. It can take values like `auto`, `none`, `visible`, and `visiblePainted`. For example, setting `pointer-events: none;` makes an element non-interactive, allowing events to pass through to the elements beneath it.

```css
.non-interactive {
  pointer-events: none;
}
```

75.What is the purpose of the CSS `box-decoration-break` property, and how can it be used with fragmented elements?

Answer:

The `box-decoration-break` property in CSS is used to control the breaking behavior of boxes when split across multiple lines. It can take values like `slice` (default) and `clone`. Setting it to `clone` ensures that the box is fully rendered on each line, while `slice` allows the box to be split, with the style applied separately to each fragment.

```
.fragmented-box {
  box-decoration-break: clone;
}
```

76.Explain the concept of the CSS `mask` property and how it can be used for image masking.

Answer:

The `mask` property in CSS is used for image masking. It allows you to apply a mask to an element, revealing only the portion of the element that is covered by the mask. The mask itself can be an image or a gradient.

```
.masked-element {
  mask: url('mask-image.png') no-repeat center / contain;
}
```

77.What is the purpose of the CSS `shape-rendering` property, and how does it affect the rendering of shapes in SVG?

Answer:

The `shape-rendering` property in CSS is used to control the rendering precision and quality of shapes in SVG images. It can take values like `auto`, `optimizeSpeed`, `crispEdges`, etc. Setting `shape-rendering: crispEdges;` ensures that shapes have crisp, well-defined edges.

```css
svg {
  shape-rendering: crispEdges;
}
```

78.Explain the CSS `user-select` property and how it can be used to control text selection.

Answer:

The `user-select` property in CSS is used to control the user's ability to select text. It can take values like `auto`, `none`, `text`, and `all`. For example, setting `user-select: none;` prevents text selection, while `user-select: all;` allows the user to select all text within an element.

```css
.unselectable {
  user-select: none;
}
```

79.What is the purpose of the CSS `scroll-behavior` property, and how does it impact scrolling behavior in a document?

Answer:

The `scroll-behavior` property in CSS is used to control the smoothness of scrolling behavior within a document. Setting `scroll-behavior: smooth;` results in a smooth animated scroll, providing a more visually appealing and user-friendly experience.

```css
html {
  scroll-behavior: smooth;
}
```

80.Explain the concept of the CSS `text-align-last` property and how it can be used to control the alignment of the last line of text.

Answer:

The `text-align-last` property in CSS is used to control the alignment of the last line of text within a block container. It can take values like `auto`, `start`, `end`, `left`, `right`, and `center`. This property is particularly useful in justified text where the last line may not fill the entire width.

```css
p {
  text-align: justify;
  text-align-last: center;
}
```

81. What is the CSS `contain: size` property, and how does it impact layout performance?

Answer:

The `contain: size` property in CSS is used to indicate that an element's size is independent of its children, allowing the browser to optimize rendering performance. It's part of the `contain` property, which also includes values like `layout`, `style`, and `paint`. By setting `contain: size;`, the browser knows that the size of the element won't be affected by changes in its content, layout, or styles.

```css
.element {
  contain: size;
}
```

82. Explain the CSS `line-clamp` property, and how can it be used to truncate multi-line text.

Answer:

The `line-clamp` property in CSS is used to truncate multi-line text and limit it to a specified number of lines. It's often used in combination with the `-webkit-line-clamp` property for compatibility with some browsers. This is commonly used for creating ellipsis-style text truncation.

```css
.multiline-text {
  display: -webkit-box;
  -webkit-line-clamp: 3; /* Number of lines to show */
  -webkit-box-orient: vertical;
  overflow: hidden;
}
```

84. Explain the concept of the CSS `object-fit` property, and how does it differ from `background-size`?

Answer:

The `object-fit` property in CSS is used to specify how a replaced element (like an image or video) should be resized to fit its container. It is similar to the `background-size` property, but it directly applies to replaced elements. Values for `object-fit` include `fill`, `contain`, `cover`, etc.

```css
img {
  object-fit: cover;
}
```

85. What is the purpose of the CSS `shape-margin` property, and how can it be used in conjunction with shapes created using `shape-outside`?

Answer:

The `shape-margin` property in CSS is used to control the margin around floated elements affected by `shape-outside`. It defines the minimum space between the element's border and the shape specified by `shape-outside`. This property helps in fine-tuning the layout around non-rectangular shapes.

```css
.shaped-element {
  float: left;
  shape-outside: circle(50%);
  shape-margin: 10px;
}
```

86. Explain the purpose of the CSS `prefers-reduced-motion` media query and how it can be used for accessibility.

Answer:

The `prefers-reduced-motion` media query in CSS is used to detect if the user has a preference for reduced motion. It can take values like `reduce` or `no-preference`. This is particularly useful for providing accessible experiences to users who may experience discomfort or motion sickness with animated content. Developers can use this query to conditionally apply styles or disable certain animations.

```css
@media (prefers-reduced-motion: reduce) {
  .animated-element {
    animation: none;
  }
}
```

87. What is the CSS `contain: paint` property, and how does it impact rendering performance?

Answer:

The `contain: paint` property in CSS is used to indicate that an element's subtree is independent of paint changes, allowing the browser to optimize rendering performance. When an element has `contain: paint;`, it signals that changes to the element won't affect the paint process, and the browser can potentially optimize rendering by isolating that subtree.

```css
.element {
  contain: paint;
}
```

88. Explain the concept of the CSS `rotate` transformation and provide an example of its usage.

Answer:

The `rotate` transformation in CSS is used to rotate an element around a specified point. It can take angles in degrees, radians, or turns. A positive angle represents a clockwise rotation, and a negative angle represents a counterclockwise rotation.

```css
.rotated-element {
  transform: rotate(45deg);
}
```

89. What is the purpose of the CSS `backdrop-filter` property, and how can it be used for creating blurred backgrounds?

Answer:

The `backdrop-filter` property in CSS is used to apply a filter effect (such as blur or brightness) to the area behind an element. It is commonly used for creating translucent or blurred backgrounds. The property supports values like `blur()`, `brightness()`, etc.

```css
.blurred-background {
  backdrop-filter: blur(8px);
}
```

90. Explain the CSS `:placeholder-shown` pseudo-class and how it can be used to style input elements based on whether the placeholder text is visible.

Answer:

The `:placeholder-shown` pseudo-class in CSS is used to select an input element based on whether its placeholder text is currently visible or not. It is often used for styling input elements differently when they are empty or when the user has entered text.

```css
input:placeholder-shown {
  border: 1px solid green;
}
```

91.What is the CSS `backface-visibility` property, and how does it impact 3D transformations?

Answer:

The `backface-visibility` property in CSS is used to determine whether the back face of an element should be visible when it is rotated in 3D space. It can take values like `visible` or `hidden`. This property is commonly used in 3D transformations to control whether the back face of an element is visible during animations.

```css
.element {
    transform: rotateY(180deg);
    backface-visibility: hidden;
}
```

92.Explain the concept of the CSS `will-change` property, and when would you use it for optimization?

Answer:

The `will-change` property in CSS is used to inform the browser that an element is expected to change in a specific way, allowing the browser to optimize the rendering process. It is often used with properties like `transform` or `opacity` that are known to trigger costly repaints or reflows. By using `will-change`, developers can hint to the browser about upcoming changes, potentially improving performance.

```css
.element {
    will-change: transform;
}
```

93.What is the purpose of the CSS `outline-offset` property, and how does it affect the positioning of outlines?

Answer:

The `outline-offset` property in CSS is used to set the space between an outline and the border edge of an element. It helps control the positioning of the outline. Positive values move the outline further from the element, and negative values move it closer.

```
.outlined-element {
  outline: 2px solid blue;
  outline-offset: 5px;
}
```

94.Explain the concept of the CSS `scroll-snap-type` property and how it can be used for creating a snapping effect during scrolling.

Answer:

The `scroll-snap-type` property in CSS is used to control the behavior of the scrolling snap points in a scroll container. It is often used in conjunction with the `scroll-snap-align` property. Setting `scroll-snap-type: mandatory;` ensures that the container snaps to each snap point during scrolling.

```
.scroll-container {
  scroll-snap-type: mandatory;
}
```

95.What is the purpose of the CSS `resize` property, and how can it be used for user interface design?

Answer:

The `resize` property in CSS is used to control whether an element is resizable by the user. It is commonly used with `<textarea>` and `<input>` elements. The property can take values like `none`, `both`, `horizontal`, and `vertical`.

```css
textarea {
  resize: both;
}
```

96.Explain the CSS `inset` shorthand property and how it simplifies the syntax for positioning.

Answer:

The `inset` shorthand property in CSS is used to set all four positioning properties (`top`, `right`, `bottom`, and `left`) in a single declaration. It simplifies the syntax for positioning elements.

```css
.box {
  inset: 10px 20px 30px 40px;
}
```

97.What is the purpose of the CSS `unicode-bidi` property, and how does it affect the bidirectional text in a document?

Answer:

The `unicode-bidi` property in CSS is used to control the handling of bidirectional text, which includes both left-to-right and right-to-left scripts. It can take values like `normal`, `embed`, and `bidi-override`. This property is important for ensuring proper rendering of text in languages that are read from right to left.

```css
.rtl-text {
  unicode-bidi: bidi-override;
}
```

98.Explain the concept of the CSS `text-overflow` property and how it can be used to handle overflow in text elements.

Answer:

   The `text-overflow` property in CSS is used to specify how the content should behave when it overflows the box in which it is contained. It is often used in conjunction with the `white-space` and `overflow` properties. The value `ellipsis` is commonly used to display an ellipsis (...) when text is truncated.


```css
.overflowing-text {
  white-space: nowrap;
  overflow: hidden;
  text-overflow: ellipsis;
}
```

99.What is the CSS `animation-fill-mode` property, and how does it impact the display of styles before and after an animation?

Answer:

   The `animation-fill-mode` property in CSS is used to control the styles applied to an element before and after the animation. It can take values like `none`, `forwards`, `backwards`, and `both`. Setting `animation-fill-mode: forwards;` ensures that the styles applied to the element persist after the animation completes.

```css
.animated-element {
  animation: slide-in 2s;
  animation-fill-mode: forwards;
}
```

100.Explain the purpose of the CSS `min-content` and `max-content` values in sizing properties.

Answer:

In CSS sizing properties like `width` or `height`, `min-content` represents the minimum size an element can be while still fitting its content, and `max-content` represents the maximum size an element can be without overflowing. These values are useful for creating flexible and responsive layouts.

```css
.element {
  width: min-content;
}
```

101.What is the CSS `initial-letter` property, and how can it be used to style the first letter of a block-level element?

Answer:

The `initial-letter` property in CSS is used to style the initial letter or letters of a block-level element. It allows you to control the styling, such as font size and color, of the first letter in a paragraph or heading.

```css
p::first-letter {
  font-size: 2em;
  color: red;
}
```

102.Explain the concept of the CSS `aspect-ratio` property, and how can it be used to create responsive containers.

Answer:

The `aspect-ratio` property in CSS is used to set the aspect ratio of an element, maintaining a specified ratio between its width and height. This is particularly useful for creating responsive containers that maintain a fixed aspect ratio regardless of the content.

```css
.responsive-container {
  aspect-ratio: 16 / 9;
}
```

103.What is the CSS `element()` function, and how can it be used in conjunction with the `mask` property?

Answer:

The `element()` function in CSS is used to reference an element in the document and use it as an image source. When combined with the `mask` property, it allows for complex masking effects using the content of another element.

```css
.masking-element {
  mask: element(#masking-source);
}
```

104.Explain the purpose of the CSS `:not()` pseudo-class, and how can it be used to select elements that do not match a specific selector.

Answer:

The `:not()` pseudo-class in CSS is used to select elements that do not match a specified selector. It is useful for applying styles to a group of elements excluding a specific subset.

```css
/* Select all paragraphs except those with class 'exclude'
p:not(.exclude) {
  color: blue;
}
```

105.What is the CSS `all` shorthand property, and how can it be used to reset styles within a rule?

Answer:

The `all` shorthand property in CSS is used to reset or remove all styles within a rule. It's often used in conjunction with the `initial` value to reset all properties to their initial/default values.

```css
.reset-styles {
  all: initial;
}
```

106.Explain the concept of the CSS `currentColor` keyword and how it can be used in conjunction with the `border` property.

Answer:

The `currentColor` keyword in CSS represents the computed value of the `color` property. It is often used in conjunction with the `border` property to dynamically apply the text color as the border color.

```css
.element {

  border: 2px solid currentColor;

}
```

107. What is the purpose of the CSS `appearance` property, and how can it be used for styling form controls?

Answer:

The `appearance` property in CSS is used to control the styling of form controls, such as buttons, checkboxes, and radio buttons. It allows you to reset the default styles provided by the browser and apply custom styles.

```css
input[type="checkbox"] {
  appearance: none;
  /* Add custom styles for checkboxes */
}
```

108. Explain the CSS `ch` unit, and how is it different from the `em` unit?

Answer:

The `ch` unit in CSS represents the width of the '0' (zero) character in the element's font. It is a relative unit, similar to `em`. However, while `em` is based on the font size of the parent element, `ch` is based on the width of the zero character.

```css
.element {
  width: 20ch;
}
```

109. What is the purpose of the CSS `hyphens` property, and how can it be used to control hyphenation in text?

Answer:

The `hyphens` property in CSS is used to control hyphenation in text when it wraps to the next line. It can take values like `auto`, `manual`, and `none`. Setting `hyphens: auto;` enables the browser to automatically hyphenate long words to improve text readability.

```css
p {
  hyphens: auto;
}
```

110. Explain the CSS `column-span` property and how it can be used to control the span of elements across multiple columns in a multi-column layout.

Answer:

The `column-span` property in CSS is used to control the span of elements across multiple columns in a multi-column layout. It can take values like `none` (default) and `all`. Setting `column-span: all;` allows an element to span across all columns.

```css
.spanning-element {
  column-span: all;
}
```

111.What is the purpose of the CSS `display: contents` property, and how does it affect the box model?

Answer:

The `display: contents` property in CSS is used to make an element's children appear as if they are direct children of the element's parent, effectively skipping the generation of the element itself in the box model. It allows the children to be laid out as if they were not contained within the element.

```css
.container {
  display: contents;
}
```

112.Explain the CSS `unset` keyword and how it can be used in property values.

Answer:

The `unset` keyword in CSS is used to reset a property to its inherited value if it inherits from its parent, or to its initial value if it does not inherit. It is often used in situations where a property needs to be explicitly reset to its default behavior.

```css
.element {
  margin: unset;
}
```

113.What is the purpose of the CSS `content-visibility` property, and how can it be used for optimizing rendering performance?

Answer:

The `content-visibility` property in CSS is used to control the rendering of content, allowing developers to skip the rendering of off-screen or hidden content until it becomes visible. It can take values like `auto` and `hidden`, and it's especially useful for optimizing performance in scenarios where not all content needs to be rendered immediately.

```css
.off-screen-content {
  content-visibility: hidden;
}
```

114.Explain the concept of the CSS `scroll-margin` property and how it can be used to create a scroll-snap effect.

Answer:

The `scroll-margin` property in CSS is used to set the margins for a scroll container, creating a "snap" effect when scrolling. It determines the distance between the scrolled-to position and the nearest snap point. This property is often used in conjunction with `scroll-snap-type`.

```css
.scroll-container {
  scroll-snap-type: y mandatory;
  scroll-margin: 20px;
}
```

115.What is the purpose of the CSS `block-size` and `inline-size` properties, and how do they differ from `width` and `height`?

Answer:

The `block-size` property in CSS is used to set the size of the block-level dimension of an element, while `inline-size` sets the size of the inline-level dimension. These properties are useful in writing mode-agnostic designs, where block and inline axes may change based on the writing mode. They are similar to `width` and `height` but adapt to the writing mode.

```css
.element {
  block-size: 200px;
  inline-size: 300px;
}
```

116.Explain the purpose of the CSS `contain: style` property and how it can be used to optimize rendering performance.

Answer:

The `contain: style` property in CSS is used to indicate that an element's styles are independent and won't affect the layout or paint of its descendants. It allows the browser to optimize rendering by isolating the styles of the contained element. This can lead to improved performance in certain scenarios.

```css
.isolated-styles {
  contain: style;
}
```

117.What is the CSS `mask-composite` property, and how can it be used in conjunction with the `mask` property for complex masking effects?

Answer:

The `mask-composite` property in CSS is used to specify how the masked image or element should be composited with the element's background. It is often used in conjunction with the `mask` property to create complex masking effects by combining multiple masks.

```css
.masked-element {
  mask: url('mask-image.svg') no-repeat center / contain;
  mask-composite: intersect;
}
```

118.Explain the concept of the CSS `shape-rendering` property and how it can affect the rendering quality of shapes in SVG.

Answer:

The `shape-rendering` property in CSS is used to control the rendering precision and quality of shapes in SVG images. It can take values like `auto`, `optimizeSpeed`, `crispEdges`, etc. Setting `shape-rendering: crispEdges;` ensures that shapes have crisp, well-defined edges.

```
svg {
    shape-rendering: crispEdges;
}
```

119.What is the purpose of the CSS `caret-color` property, and how can it be used to style the color of the text cursor (caret) in an input or textarea?

Answer:

The `caret-color` property in CSS is used to set the color of the text cursor (caret) in an input or textarea element. It allows developers to customize the appearance of the caret, making it more visible or aligned with the overall design.

```
input {
    caret-color: red;
}
```

120.Explain the CSS `place-items` property and how it can be used in conjunction with grid or flex containers for shorthand placement of items.

Answer:

The `place-items` property in CSS is a shorthand property that sets both the `align-items` and `justify-items` properties in a single declaration. It is often used with grid or flex containers to quickly set the alignment of items along both the block and inline axes.

```css
.grid-container {
  display: grid;
  place-items: center;
}
```

121.What is the purpose of the CSS `font-variant` property, and how does it affect text styling?

Answer:

The `font-variant` property in CSS is used to control the styling of font variants for text. It can take values like `normal` or `small-caps`. When set to `small-caps`, the font is displayed with small capital letters for uppercase characters.

```
p {
    font-variant: small-caps;
}
```

122.Explain the concept of the CSS `translate()` transformation, and how can it be used to move an element in the 2D plane?

Answer:

The `translate()` transformation in CSS is used to move an element in the 2D plane. It takes two parameters, `tx` for the horizontal translation and `ty` for the vertical translation. Positive values move the element right and down, while negative values move it left and up.

```
.translated-element {
    transform: translate(20px, 30px);
}
```

123.What is the purpose of the CSS `scroll-behavior` property, and how does it impact scrolling behavior in a document?

Answer:

The `scroll-behavior` property in CSS is used to control the smoothness of scrolling behavior within a document. Setting `scroll-behavior: smooth;` results in a smooth animated scroll, providing a more visually appealing and user-friendly experience.

```css
html {
  scroll-behavior: smooth;
}
```

124.Explain the CSS `word-wrap` property and its role in handling long words or strings that may overflow their container.

Answer:

The `word-wrap` property in CSS is used to control whether long words or strings should be broken and wrap onto the next line when they exceed the width of their container. Setting `word-wrap: break-word;` allows words to break and wrap to prevent overflow.

```css
.long-text {
  word-wrap: break-word;
}
```

125.What is the purpose of the CSS `font-feature-settings` property, and how can it be used to enable or disable font features?

Answer:

The `font-feature-settings` property in CSS is used to enable or disable font features, such as ligatures or alternate character forms. It takes values like `"liga"` (ligatures), `"dlig"` (discretionary ligatures), etc. This property allows for fine control over typographic features.

```
p {
    font-feature-settings: "liga" on;
}
```

126.Explain the CSS `line-height` property, and how does it impact the spacing between lines of text within an element?

Answer:

The `line-height` property in CSS is used to set the height of a line box within an element, affecting the spacing between lines of text. It can be set as a unitless number, a percentage, or a length. A value of `1.5` means the line height is 1.5 times the font size.

```
p {
    line-height: 1.5;
}
```

127.What is the purpose of the CSS `page-break` properties (`page-break-before`, `page-break-after`, and `page-break-inside`), and how can they be used for controlling page breaks in printed documents?

Answer:

The `page-break` properties in CSS (`page-break-before`, `page-break-after`, and `page-break-inside`) are used to control page breaks in printed documents. They determine whether a page break should occur before, after, or inside a specified element.

```
.page-break-after {
    page-break-after: always;
}
```

128.Explain the CSS `will-change: transform` property and its role in optimizing performance for animated transformations.

Answer:

The `will-change: transform` property in CSS is used to inform the browser that an element is expected to change in a way that involves the `transform` property. This allows the browser to optimize the rendering process, resulting in improved performance during animations.

```css
.animating-element {
  will-change: transform;
}
```

129.What is the CSS `scroll-padding` property, and how can it be used to control the padding around scroll containers?

Answer:

The `scroll-padding` property in CSS is used to set the padding around scroll containers. It ensures that when scrolling to a specific target, there is a specified amount of space left around the target within the scroll container.

```css
.scroll-container {
  scroll-padding: 20px;
}
```

130.Explain the purpose of the CSS `overscroll-behavior` property and its values (`auto`, `contain`, `none`).

Answer:

The `overscroll-behavior` property in CSS is used to control the behavior of the user agent when the user overscrolls the viewport or a scroll container. It can take values like `auto`, `contain`, and `none`. For example, setting `overscroll-behavior: none;` prevents the browser from showing the default overscroll effect.

```css
.scroll-container {
  overscroll-behavior: none;
}
```

131.What is the purpose of the CSS `box-decoration-break` property, and how does it affect the styling of broken elements (e.g., across columns or pages)?

Answer:

The `box-decoration-break` property in CSS is used to control how the styles of an element should be applied when the element is broken across multiple lines, columns, or pages. It can take values like `slice` or `clone`. `slice` allows the element to be broken, and its styles are applied separately to each fragment, while `clone` copies the styles for each fragment.

```css
.broken-element {
  box-decoration-break: clone;
}
```

132.Explain the concept of the CSS `currentColor` keyword and how it can be used to dynamically inherit the color value of an element.

Answer:

The `currentColor` keyword in CSS is used to dynamically inherit the computed value of the `color` property of an element. It is often used in properties that accept color values, allowing them to automatically inherit the color from the surrounding context.

```
.colored-border {
  border: 2px solid currentColor;
}
```

133.What is the purpose of the CSS `column-fill` property, and how does it affect the distribution of content in multi-column layouts?

Answer:

The `column-fill` property in CSS is used to control how content is distributed between columns in a multi-column layout. It can take values like `auto` or `balance`. Setting `column-fill: balance;` attempts to distribute content evenly across columns, creating a balanced layout.

```
.multi-column-container {
  column-fill: balance;
}
```

134.Explain the CSS `inset` shorthand property and how it can be used for setting the values of `top`, `right`, `bottom`, and `left` in a single declaration.

Answer:

The `inset` shorthand property in CSS is used to set the values of `top`, `right`, `bottom`, and `left` properties in a single declaration. It simplifies the syntax for positioning elements by specifying all four values at once.

```css
.positioned-element {
  inset: 10px 20px 30px 40px;
}
```

135.What is the purpose of the CSS `image-rendering` property, and how can it be used to control the rendering quality of images in a browser?

Answer:

The `image-rendering` property in CSS is used to control the rendering quality of images in a browser. It can take values like `auto`, `pixelated`, or `crisp-edges`. Setting `image-rendering: pixelated;` can be useful for preserving the pixelated appearance of low-resolution images.

```css
img {
  image-rendering: pixelated;
}
```

136.Explain the concept of the CSS `clip-path` property and how it can be used to create non-rectangular shapes by clipping elements.

Answer:

The `clip-path` property in CSS is used to create non-rectangular shapes by defining a clipping region. It can take values like `circle()`, `polygon()`, or `ellipse()`. This property is commonly used for creating complex shapes or applying visual effects.

```css
.custom-shape {
  clip-path: polygon(0 0, 100% 0, 100% 80%, 0 100%);
}
```

137.What is the purpose of the CSS `all: unset` property, and how can it be used to reset all properties within a rule to their initial values?

Answer:

The `all: unset` property in CSS is used to reset all properties within a rule to their initial values. It effectively removes all styles applied to the element and allows developers to start with a clean slate.

```css
.reset-styles {
  all: unset;
}
```

138.Explain the concept of the CSS `writing-mode` property and how it can be used to control the directionality of text and layout in a document.

Answer:

The `writing-mode` property in CSS is used to control the directionality of text and layout in a document. It can take values like `horizontal-tb`, `vertical-rl`, or `vertical-lr`. This property is essential for handling scripts that are written in vertical or right-to-left orientations.

```css
.vertical-text {
  writing-mode: vertical-rl;
}
```

139.What is the purpose of the CSS `contain: layout` property, and how can it be used to optimize layout performance?

Answer:

The `contain: layout` property in CSS is used to indicate that an element's subtree is independent of layout changes, allowing the browser to optimize rendering performance. When an element has `contain: layout;`, it signals that changes to the layout won't affect the rest of the document, and the browser can potentially optimize layout calculations.

```css
.layout-optimized {
  contain: layout;
}
```

140.Explain the CSS `outline-style` property and its values (`dotted`, `dashed`, `solid`).

Answer:

The `outline-style` property in CSS is used to set the style of the outline around an element. It can take values like `dotted`, `dashed`, or `solid`. This property is commonly used in conjunction with `outline-color` and `outline-width` to customize the appearance of outlines.

```css
.outlined-element {
  outline-style: dashed;
}
```

141.What is the purpose of the CSS `empty-cells` property, and how can it be used to control the display of borders around empty table cells?

Answer:

The `empty-cells` property in CSS is used to control the display of borders around empty cells in a table. It can take values like `show` or `hide`. Setting `empty-cells: hide;` hides the borders around empty cells, while `empty-cells: show;` displays them.

```css
table {
  empty-cells: hide;
}
```

142.Explain the CSS `tab-size` property and how it can be used to control the width of tab characters in text.

Answer:

The `tab-size` property in CSS is used to control the width of tab characters in text. It specifies the number of spaces that a tab character should represent. It's useful for maintaining consistent indentation in code or text.

```css
pre {
  tab-size: 4;
}
```

143.What is the purpose of the CSS `unicode-range` descriptor in the `@font-face` rule, and how can it be used to define specific ranges of Unicode characters for a font?

Answer:

The `unicode-range` descriptor in the `@font-face` rule is used to define specific ranges of Unicode characters for which a font file should be applied. It allows for the selective loading of font resources based on the characters used on a webpage.

```css
@font-face {
  font-family: 'CustomFont';
  src: url('custom-font.woff2') format('woff2');
  unicode-range: U+0025-00FF; /* Specifies the range of characters */
}
```

144.Explain the CSS `contain: paint` property and its role in optimizing the painting phase of rendering.

Answer:

The `contain: paint` property in CSS is used to indicate that an element's subtree is independent of the painting phase, allowing the browser to optimize the painting performance. It signals that changes to the element won't affect the rest of the document during the painting phase.

```css
.paint-optimized {
  contain: paint;
}
```

145.What is the CSS `transition-timing-function` property, and how does it impact the speed of a CSS transition between two states?

Answer:

The `transition-timing-function` property in CSS is used to specify the speed curve of a transition between two states. It can take values like `ease`, `linear`, `ease-in`, `ease-out`, etc. This property controls the acceleration and deceleration of the transition, affecting its overall timing.

```css
.transition-element {
  transition-timing-function: ease-in-out;
}
```

146.Explain the concept of the CSS `all` shorthand property and how it can be used to reset multiple properties to their initial values.

Answer:

The `all` shorthand property in CSS is used to reset multiple properties to their initial values within a rule. It is often used with the value `initial` to clear all styles applied to an element.

```css
.reset-styles {
  all: initial;
}
```

147.What is the purpose of the CSS `min-block-size` and `min-inline-size` properties, and how do they differ from `min-height` and `min-width`?

Answer:

The `min-block-size` property in CSS is used to set the minimum block size of an element, while `min-inline-size` sets the minimum inline size. These properties are similar to `min-height` and `min-width` but adapt to the writing mode, making them suitable for responsive design regardless of the writing mode.

```css
.element {
  min-block-size: 100px;
  min-inline-size: 150px;
}
```

148.Explain the CSS `box-sizing` property and its values (`content-box` and `border-box`).

Answer:

The `box-sizing` property in CSS is used to control how the size of an element is calculated, including padding and borders. It can take values like `content-box` (default) or `border-box`. With `border-box`, the width and height include padding and border, simplifying layout calculations.

```css
.border-box-element {
  box-sizing: border-box;
}
```

149.What is the purpose of the CSS `object-fit` property, and how can it be used to control the sizing and scaling of replaced elements like images and videos?

Answer:

The `object-fit` property in CSS is used to control how replaced elements (like images and videos) should be sized and scaled within their containing box. It can take values like `fill`, `contain`, `cover`, etc.

```css
img {
  object-fit: cover;
}
```

150.Explain the concept of the CSS `mask-type` property and how it can be used to define the masking behavior of an element with an SVG image mask.

Answer:

The `mask-type` property in CSS is used to define the masking behavior of an element with an SVG image mask. It can take values like `luminance` or `alpha`. `mask-type: luminance;` indicates that the SVG mask is applied based on the luminance values of the mask image.

```css
.masked-element {
  mask-type: luminance;
}
```